"For over three we[...]
me while I edited her [...]
Finish Rich." When I received the manuscript to read, I was excited about her ideas, the easy writing style and interesting stories. I instantly felt connected, as I know the subject well. I had an immediate urge to help her with the final editing.

I feel that the book is written based on Edna's professional and personal experiences, with honest emotions that come from the heart.

I absolutely love the many practical suggestions that turn complex processes into easy steps, as well as the many lovely stories illustrating the various theories that make the examples so real.

The book is warmly written, which makes it a pleasant read that talks directly to the reader. It is addressed mainly to women but I am sure that all genders will benefit from it."

Helen Sher, Accountant and
Registered Tax Agent

II

EDNA FERMAN

STRONG WOMEN FINISH RICH

A powerful plan to live an extraordinary life

Ferman, Edna
Strong Women Finish Rich – A powerful plan to live an extraordinary life

Cover design: Black Card Books
Cover picture: Zohar Izenberg
Internal design by Edna Ferman

ISBN 978-1-64606-071-9
First edition, April 2020

TO MY PARENTS

Rina & the late Dan Yancovitch

for raising me with love,
passion for learning
and creativity

Contents

Foreword

By Edna Schur-Rubinstein, CEO, Founder and Visionary of Re-Source Institute International

When I was invited to read Edna Ferman's book and consider writing a forward, I knew that it was a special invite, as our lives' paths tend to cross and meet often. I was keen to read the book and since I have known that Edna's coaching and seminar materials always made an impact on myself and on others, I was thrilled to accept it.

I met Edna Ferman in 2009, when I was-studying Traditional Chinese Medicine (TCM) in Australia. At the time I was organizing a systemic[1] workshop and I was looking for a suitable hall in which to run it in. While searching for the right location, I was introduced to Edna Ferman, who was the president of her community's club, and had the venue I was looking for.

The interesting thing was, both our names are Edna. We had an immediate connection, and even more so, we also had emotional and physical similarities especially her daughter and I. Long story short we became friends. Edna Ferman had just finished her coaching education and we coached each other in various areas of life, had deep discussions about life, development, and growth and when time came for me to move back to Europe and get married in Israel, she came and celebrated with me.

Following my studies in TCM, including: Genetic Mutations, Epigenetics, Healing and Functional Medicine, I opened an Interdisciplinary Health Center in Switzerland in 2015. With new partners added, we are launching our new company in May 2020:
"Re-Source Institute" - the first Functional Medicine Institute in Switzerland and Europe.
Re-source Institute will include a premium health center, a luxury retreat, the "Academy for Open Minded Medicine" and a re-source health podcast, where Edna Ferman will contribute towards it.

When, in January 2019 when Edna told me that she was writing a book and that she had studied Recall Healing, part of which is a generational healing, I was flabbergasted. WOW, this was such an amazing timing again, as that was the subject that connected us in the first place – and everything comes full circle again.

You are a winner! Sit with this sentence for a moment.
You are a winner!
Why? Because, you are this one sperm who made it through the competition of multiple million others into the one egg. For that reason, YOU are the winner and you have an absolute crucial purpose in your life, to fulfill your path and your dreams.
If you are a woman, then you are a super-human by choice!

Through history men feared women and therefore subdued them. Today with the emancipation and awakening of the new woman "species", we women have a major role-in the world, and for humanity.

In Edna's book "Strong Women Finish Rich" it is not only about finishing rich in money, but the main message is to allow women to acknowledge their internal richness. Reaching internal richness happens through development and growth and by understanding that we don't need to hold onto family loyalties, which hold us back. We don't need to repeat our ancestor's history or carry their pain.

For this book, Edna has researched through her own and her family's journey, and enfolded her knowledge into stories, which makes this book so special. In the 9 chapters of her book, you will go through an internal journey of figuring out who you are. Discover why it is worth it to really love yourself, to overcome the obstacles that hinder you and to follow your heart. To acknowledge what holds you back, and are you giving yourself permission to do so? As YOU play the main role in your life. When you understand that you are the one making your choices, your whole life perspective will change.
All aspects of your life will change and you will be able to pave the road to your personal future, the way you want it. The best gift is, that you can pass it on to your children and grandchildren.

Edna really hit the mark, by writing this book and opening the internal and external eyes of many women. To every woman reading this book I can deeply recommend Edna's coaching programs, where you can reach a deeper level of understanding and transformation.

Edna asked me to write her Foreword, not just because we have the same name, but mainly because both of us are strong women. We both have gone through an internal transformation and learned not just, "not to give up", but to do an internal search for a better path of our personal journey and to live our dreams.

For the future of my vision for "Re-Source Institute", Edna will be part of it in Australia, where she can transform many more women and make the world a better place.

I hope you will enjoy reading this book, as much as I did, and find your way to being a strong and rich woman.

Resourceful wishes,

Edna Schur-Rubinstein
Zurich 2020
www.re-source.care

Introduction

I was asked by my friend to talk to her daughter and help her with some personal challenges. The daughter had a successful executive job at the bank, but in her personal life, her relationship was going sour. The daughter was happy to meet with me and we went for a coffee to see if I could be of any help.

After two hours of stories and discussions, my friend's daughter stood up and said "Edna, I've decided you are going to be a coach!" I just looked at her with astonishment and didn't know exactly what to say. She added that she had a life coach at the bank, and since she works as a professional in human resources, she knows how to identify strengths in people. From my approach, she could see that I had the qualities of a coach.

It took me completely by surprise. Even though I always helped people with their finances and in different challenges of life, I never thought about becoming a coach.

It wasn't the first time someone suggested I do certain things, and in my experience, the suggestions were almost always right. So I decided to look into coaching. I received from my friend's daughter the name and the phone number of the coach from the bank and I also knew someone that was coaching executives and business people. I contacted them both and enquired about coaching in general and about their work and experience.

The fascinating part was that those two coaches studied at the same coaching school. I enquired about it and was informed that their coaching course was based on neuroscience; how the brain works.
It sounded interesting. Since I was a child I've always been attracted to psychology, reading and learning about different aspects and theories. I was really attracted to that subject. It was what I was always reading and learning about.

A week later, the daughter called me and asked how I was doing and I told her that she had given me a lot of work. I told her that I had enquired about coaching and enrolled in a course.

And, as we say, the rest is history. I finished the course, became accredited, and over the years I have coached hundreds of women, and I've loved every minute of it. I especially love seeing the change and transformation of my clients. Lately, I added "healing" to my professional services, complimenting the "mentoring" and "coaching" services for complete wellbeing and successful achievements.

There is a purpose to our lives, but often it's hidden from us. It only makes sense when we look back and see the reasons for our bigger challenges, heartbreaks, or "derailing." It never makes sense in the moment we're experiencing them. And sometimes, our biggest "presents" arrive with an unexpected wrapping (just like the present of my friend's daughter suggesting that I be a coach).

My working journey started in a completely different field - in the world of Importing and Distributing car parts. I usually have to repeat it, when people ask about my history, since it is so different than coaching.

I entered that business without planning. When my husband started the import business, he needed help in answering the phone, correspondence, writing invoices, and managing the office. It was a natural way for me to help in the business, and every day I got further involved and needed more. In no time at all, I was a Managing Director, and as the business grew, my part as a partner grew too. I have been fortunate to have a successful business and career, going each day to work with joy and pleasure.

Twenty-five years later, after selling my part of the business, I had some time for myself and I enjoyed the freedom of not going to work every day. As every businessperson knows, it's nearly impossible to get the business bug out of you.

I was in a new space looking for new opportunities, using my business knowledge and experience.

I have ventured into Real-Estate investments and Internet Marketing. I enjoyed those business activities, but I was missing the every day interaction with people.

Reflecting on my intuition, I have always trusted my intuition and feelings. Since this approach has never let me down, when I was offered the idea to be a life coach, I put my trust in my feelings that indicated an exciting future of coaching people to achieve more in their lives, and I decided to follow that path. I believe that everyone has to trust in something: guts, feelings, destiny, or the universe. When you learn to listen to your own feelings, you follow the path that is right for you. I always say, "Your feelings never lie." I believed in my feelings for my entire adult life, and it has made all the difference in my experience.

I never thought I would write a book. I am not a scholar or a journalist, but I wanted to gather my thoughts, wisdom, and the lessons I shared in my mentoring and coaching sessions, so I decided to write a book.

Talking to hundreds of women and listening to their small and big struggles, my aim was to steer them to new insights and understandings and enable them to acquire new strengths that translate into a rich and powerful life. Through my practice, I realized that their paths to their new insights are important valuable lessons for other women to acquire.
These insights can change and transform lives from struggle to splendor.

I am not a therapist, this book is about sharing the lessons I've learned, the pearls of wisdom I've assembled, and inspiring stories I've gathered to enable you to create a life filled with purpose and meaning. It's about empowering you to shine and enjoy an extraordinary life.

This book is designed to help you move forward and actually do it. As I know that this is not a simple matter, I incorporated different processes, plans, tools, and easy practical practices to engage with, which will enable you to achieve the best possible version of YOU.

My goal is to see you becoming a strong woman, a woman that has the aptitude to live her life to the fullest and achieve an extraordinary life.

This book was created for your success, for you to become a strong woman and finish rich. In this book, I am sharing ideas, lessons, and pearls of wisdom, stories, wonder, wellbeing, harmony, and strength.

Many of those ideas and lessons have revealed themselves to me while Coaching and Mentoring. They've frequently surfaced during sessions. I added to them some stories and tools, in order to enhance new understandings and preserving them.

What does it mean to be a strong woman?

I have asked many women that same question and the reply was varied. To some, being a strong woman meant to have a strong will or be financially stable, and to others it meant to live life powerfully, to live each day to the fullest, or to have strong relationships and a satisfying career.

Whatever "strong woman" means to you, I hope you will enjoy this book and the ideas I am sharing. To some, the ideas can be strange at first. To others not all the ideas will appear real or acceptable. Others will embrace and appreciate the thoughts, philosophies, viewpoints, concepts, and beliefs from the start.

So what is a rich woman?

Is it a woman with a good income or possessions and assets, or is it a woman with strength of character, which can manage her life with love, happiness, enthusiasm, and pure enjoyment of great relationships with family and friends?

It is your choice to decide what a rich woman means to you, how rich you would like to be, or where wealth will lie. From experience, I know that you can't enjoy your physical "richness," wealth in assets and possessions, without having a rich and fulfilling emotional life.

From my experience, fulfilment and love are the foundations of what we need and want in our lives.

This book was created for **YOU!**

I hope that by considering the thoughts and ideas in this book, you will be able to create the image of the woman you wish to be, live your life as a **STRONG WOMAN** and **FINISH RICH**.

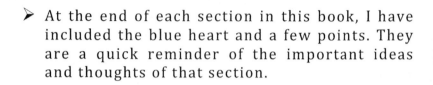

➤ At the end of each section in this book, I have included the blue heart and a few points. They are a quick reminder of the important ideas and thoughts of that section.

➤ The blue heart symbolizes a deep and stable love, trust, harmony, peace and loyalty. I have chosen it for you, to use these points with peace and harmony.

Edna Ferman
Sydney, 2020

Make a decision for
a better life
And don't look back.
Your time is *NOW!*

Chapter 1

Treat Yourself as Gold

1.1 Love Yourself First -
if you never try, you'll never know.

"Treat yourself as gold" is not typically a thought that comes to women's minds regularly or frequently. Often it's not even in our vocabulary.

Life is too fast, busy hectic and full. I never thought about it over the years, but I had a certain protective mechanism for myself - a way to protect myself so I can continue my busy and sometimes hectic life of looking after my family, developing my business, as well as engaging in a big project of renovation and building our home. In order to conserve my energy, I developed "breathing stops."

I created "breathing stops" for my wellbeing, and existence. The "breathing stops" were created when I felt that I needed a break, a break for few minutes, an hour, a day, or a weekend. I needed some relief from the pressures of life, the pressure of attending to my family's needs, busy times at work and building the house.

I needed the "breathing stops" as exclusive time for myself, to stop and recharge my batteries. I just knew that I needed them in order to preserve my vitality, and for my soul.

My "breathing stops" were varied. Some mornings, before going to work, I would go to a shopping center, have a look around, and have morning tea before going to my office. On other occasions, I would go shopping for few hours, just to have a bit of a break from the pressure of work and family life.

Many times when I left work exhausted after a very busy day, I would go to a local coffee shop, have a rest for 15-30 minutes, drink a cup of coffee with a snack, read the newspaper or a magazine, and just rest and relax. After getting my energy back, I was ready to go home to my family - "to my second job" as I used to call it - and cook dinner, help with homework and enjoy our family time together.

I thought that it was better to arrive home relaxed, and to attend to my family needs, rather than worn-out and stressed out from a busy day at work.

Not sure how this knowledge came to me - maybe it came to me out of necessity. I knew that I needed this protective mechanism but didn't see it as "treating" myself. Only years later, when I coached women on how to love themselves, I realized the significance of it. I realized that somehow I learned to treat myself as gold.

I realized that I had been treating myself in other ways, too. The renovation and building new sections of our house were done while we lived there. At times after a hectic period of building and a completion of a certain stage, my husband and I would go to a hotel in the city for a night or two, just to unload some of the pressure we were experiencing, especially from living in a building site with various trades people working around us.

At the time, it was a necessity for both my husband and myself, and only years later did I understand that I was working on "loving myself first" in order to be able to share my love with my family.

I grew up in a traditional home. My parents both worked, which was not very common at that time in other countries around the world. In those days, women were typically stay-at-home moms. I grew up in Israel, where many women were working outside their homes. Compared to many other countries, Israel was a more equal society.

By the mid-eighties, the world had evolved. Girls were more educated and were taught that they had choices and could achieve anything that they desired: a good education, a career, as well as motherhood.

11

They were told that they could have it all.

Integrating professional and personal aspirations seemed very easy and possible. So many women advanced in their professions and also fulfilled their responsibilities at home with their family. Their partners didn't usually share the load of housework and child rearing, and as a result, many women found themselves working two full-time jobs.

In time, women realized that it was far more challenging than they envisioned. They learned that sometimes something had to give in order to "have it all." Without much time to think or plan, many women neglected the most important person in the family: herself.

As they devote their lives to their kids, husbands, housework, and work and to all who needed their help and support, they actually forgot about their own needs, wishes, and desires.

Women usually don't prioritize their own needs until they deplete themselves of all energy and their lives come to a halt. They arrive at a point where they have no other choice. They start to look for solutions for managing their lives so that their family, work, and especially their souls will live together in harmony.

"Love yourself first" is often not in the conscious mind of women. The best way to get started on this path is to fall in love with yourself FIRST.

It's not always easy, especially if we have had life experiences that didn't encourage us to love ourselves. If we didn't grow up with love, sometimes it's not easy to know how to love ourselves. But loving yourself can be a learned practice.

To "love yourself first" is to consider yourself as a member of your family who needs love and affection, other needs, requirements, and desires.

You are a family member that has to be happy and fulfilled, just like all your other family members. And you are a special member of the family, looking after the whole family, so why shouldn't you be looked after too?

Occasionally people look at me oddly when I convey to them the idea of "love yourself first" or question the notion of being number one. Many women have no awareness of the value of this mindset and are not always open to comprehend and accept this change in perspective.

In my business, at times, I used to tell my colleagues "I am NUMBER ONE." They would often look at me with astonishment, as if to say: How can it be? What about your kids? Aren't they number one? My explanation was that I needed to look after myself first in order to look after my family.

To illustrate further, think about traveling on a plane. Before taking off, the flight attendant reads the emergency instructions and states that in the case of an emergency, always put the oxygen mask on yourself first *before* putting it on your child.

Here is an instance of looking after yourself first in order to be able to look after your kids.

"Love yourself first" is not an occasional treat, and it's not a selfish behaviour. It is a necessity to enable us to care for others, to care for ourselves, and to live well.

At various coaching sessions and at my seminars, I talk frequently about the notion of "love yourself first" and the concept of "I am number one." At times I saw a number of participants looking at me with big, open eyes. In those instances, I knew that I should explain these concepts further and give examples, as these thoughts are not very common. And sometimes, as some participants told me, only after listening to me explaining it a few times does a new understanding appear. As "love yourself first" and "I am number one" are concepts often associated with selfish behavior.

I remember being told, "You were telling me to be number one for years, but I never understood it, as it sounded very selfish. Only today I got it. Suddenly, I understood what you meant all those years."

- ✓ *Love Yourself FIRST!*
- ✓ *NEVER criticize yourself*
- ✓ *Be gentle with yourself*
- ✓ *LOVE YOURSELF EVERYDAY*
- ✓ *Treat yourself as GOLD*
- ✓ *YOU Deserve It!*

The biggest issue for women is: put yourself first.
So much time is spent on the kids, husband and
housework and by the end of the day there is nothing
to give to yourself.
No one else would put your needs first,
if you don't, who will?"

Alice - KinesiAlice
www.kinesialice.com.au

Fall in love with yourself
Every day

1.2 You Are Unique

Has Anyone Told You?

Each of us was born with gifts. Our gifts are our talents. Not everyone receives the same gifts. Sometimes we have to stop, look within ourselves and appreciate our gifts. Our gifts are often the activities we excel in and most enjoy participating in: the things we gladly invest our hours and days in. These gifts can come in the form of music, reading, business, painting, math, computer work, cooking, writing, sculpture, singing, teaching, etc.

Our talents are all different. It doesn't matter how clever, beautiful or capable you are, we all have certain talents and that's what makes us unique. You are born with some talents, and other talents you develop over the years, or perhaps you just discover them when you realize one day that you are good at something you didn't know you were good at.

Everyone has an awareness of his or her unique abilities – that is, in what area they naturally excel. Some individuals do no appreciate their abilities and talents. Sometimes, they might believe that everyone has the same talents and that they are not unique. We often don't realize that not everyone is the same. Not everyone performs the way you do in work or life.

17

My gifts are mentoring, coaching and painting. Those are three areas of my life that I can spend hours and days doing what I love with great enjoyment and without noticing the time pass. Interestingly enough, I discovered these passions at a later stage of my life.

When I turned 30, I knew that I wanted to paint. From a young age I enjoyed arts and crafts; however, between my business and caring for my family, I was unable to find the peace of mind and the time to paint. I never thought that I would paint, as I am not good at drawing, but somehow without explanation I wanted to paint.

Many years later, after I sold my share of my business, time became more available to me and I started painting. I love painting and since drawing isn't one of my gifts, my style is to create abstract paintings.

It's important to think about our gifts and discover them. As children some of us discover them at an early age, like being good at reading, drawing, excelling at a certain sport, and for others, the discoveries appear at a later age.

What are your gifts?

What would you like to do for your

enjoyment?

Sometimes it takes time to discover them. They are wrapped gifts that are waiting for a special date or event to be unwrapped and discovered.

But if you have an urge to do something for your enjoyment, for "your soul," and it is possible for you to do it, even if it takes some effort, take the steps to uncover your gifts. Enjoy them and celebrate your uniqueness. You don't have to uncover any big talents, as anything you do with enjoyment and success is a gift. Even the ability to make people feel good or smile is a gift too.

The Cracked Pot

An old Chinese woman carried two pots from the well to her home every day. One pot had a crack and the other was perfect. The perfect pot arrived everyday full of water to the woman's home, and the cracked pot arrived half full.

For two years, the woman brought home one pot full of water while the other was half full. The full pot was very proud of his achievements, but the cracked one was upset and unhappy with his imperfection, since he achieved only half of his objective.

Two years of carrying water passed, and the cracked pot considered itself to be a complete failure. He looked at the woman and said: "I am ashamed of myself, I would like to apologize to you." "Why?" asked the woman. He continued, "I am upset about my imperfection and that every day for the last two years, the crack I have is losing half the water along the way to your home."

The old woman smiled and replied, "Did you notice the beautiful flowers on your side of the path? There are no flowers on the other side.

I noticed your imperfection a long time ago, so I planted flower seeds on your side of the path, and everyday when you carry the water, you water them.

For the last two years, I have cut the beautiful flowers, brought them home, put them on the table, and enjoyed a lovely room."

We all have some imperfections; our cracks and blemishes make us special and unique.

Your gifts are part of you. Appreciate your gifts, be proud of them, and don't be afraid to use them with pride and demonstrate them. Appreciate your uniqueness and express yourself!

- ➢ Appreciate your gifts
- ➢ Enjoy your special gifts
- ➢ You are unique
- ➢ Appreciate your uniqueness

You are original
No one else in the world
is like

YOU!

1.3 It's Your Life

It's Your Life! It consists of love, happiness, success, sadness, disappointments, or lack there of. It is your life and you are the one who is in charge and in control of it.

We often tend to blame other people or events for circumstances that have occurred in our lives. At times, it's not up to us and we are involved in circumstances that affect us while we have no say, no choice and no ability to change them. But there are also parts of your life that you *can* influence and change. In these circumstances, you are the only one responsible for your life, and you are the only one who can create change. No one else can create any change for you. Change won't happen if you don't want it or are not ready for it.

It's all about decisions and how you perceive or want to see your life. It's up to you, and you choose what you would like to bring into your life, like happiness, success, freedom, love, or something else. You can shut the door when you see the negative thoughts and feelings trying to sneak into your mind and your life, such as sadness, anger, loneliness, or others. When they try to come into your life, you have the power to deny them entry.

You are the only one in control of your life. If you give your control to others, you will live according to their rules.

It's your life, you have the power to create it the way you want it, and you are the only one with this power. Use it and create the life you dream of. It is your choice to change it whenever you want.

It reminds me of the story I often like to share - the story *"Why the Elephants Don't Run Away"*:

I still remember the traveling circus that used to go from city to city and come from overseas to show off their animals and their special acts including clowns and acrobats.

When I was a young girl, I used to love going to see the circus that came to town. My biggest joy was to see the animals: the lions, tigers, monkeys, and elephants! The elephants were the most amazing animals. I also knew of other kids that loved the elephants, as they were large, heavy, and strong.

I noticed that between performances, those huge creatures were held only by a chain tied to their front leg.

The trainer used to tie the chain from the elephant's front leg to a small hook that was inserted into the ground.

The hook was just a wooden peg that was inserted only few centimeters in the ground. Even though the chain was thick and strong, for such a strong animal that could pull trees out of the ground without much effort, it looked like he could definitely release himself easily from that hook and run away.

I was confused by the fact that the elephants, being such strong creatures that could definitely break free from their peg easily, did not run away.

And I wondered: Why is the elephant still there? Why doesn't he run away?

One day when I saw a trainer nearby, I asked why these big and mighty animals just stood there and made no attempt to escape. The trainer told me that elephants don't run away because they are trained.

So my next question was: If they are trained, why are they tied to the hook?

And the answer was:

The elephants don't run away from the circus because they have been tied to the hook from an early age.

I closed my eyes and tried to imagine the little elephant tied to the hook. The trainer told me that small elephants tried to release themselves from the hook that controlled them but they couldn't.

I started imagining how the small elephant pulled and pushed, perspired, and tried again and again to get free. But after many trials he couldn't be freed – it was impossible. It was beyond his efforts.

I imagined again how he was trying day after day, and by the end of each day, he fell asleep exhausted. Until one day, which was a sad day for the elephant, he gave up... and accepted his fate.

The big and mighty elephants that we saw in the circus didn't escape because they *believed* that they COULDN'T escape. Their inability to escape when they were very small was etched in their memory, so they never ever thought to try again. They never tried again to check their strength...

Like the elephants in the circus, how many of us go through life tied to one or more hooks and are hanging onto old beliefs that are stopping us from achieving in life, simply because we failed at it earlier? How many of us are held back by old, outdated beliefs that no longer serve us?

Maybe you are convinced of the fact that you "can't" do certain things. Maybe because you tried them in the past when you were younger, you still believe that you are not capable or that success would be impossible. You might be like the elephants and think that you cannot and will never be able to do, change, or achieve.

Some of us grew up with a message of "I can't." It's a message that you may have heard from your parents, teachers or anyone else and you believed them. You trusted those people, adopted that belief and it became a part of you, your "Truth." And ultimately, you never ever gave yourself the chance to try again.

You can live with your "Truth" all your life, or you can change it. The only way to know if you can succeed is to try again, as you are the only one with the power to change and improve your life.

For the second time I came across this incident with two different people. One incident was a few years ago and the second one, happened just recently. A member of my family, that was unable to grasp math at school, gave up learning it at high school.

28

Recently, years later, math was a pre requisite for a course she wanted to study at university. She took up a math course, with the same material she couldn't comprehend when she was younger and she was amazed to see her perfect marks at the end of the course.

This was a result of overcoming a limiting belief: "I am not good at math." My family member did her utmost and didn't succumb to her childhood belief.

As a result, she didn't stay tied to the hook, like the elephant, for the rest of her life.

- ➢ You can always change your beliefs!
- ➢ Challenge your beliefs
- ➢ You can create your life
- ➢ Which belief would you like to change TODAY?
- ➢ What are you inviting into your life TODAY?

It only takes one person
To change your life...
YOU!

1.4 Your Opportunities

Opportunities in life are gifts. They are presented to us in different shapes and sizes. They are presented at different times and situations. They are not always clear and they don't always necessarily look like opportunities.

Sometimes it's easy to dismiss them only to learn later that they were amazing opportunities. When we don't embrace them, they just disappear, and we never know what great opportunities were available to us.

Embrace every invitation or request you receive for an event, a meeting, or volunteer opportunity, as you never know whom you will meet that will influence you to change your life. Embrace every opportunity to help someone, as you never know what gift you'll get out of it.

There have been times in my life when I thought that I was helping someone, but actually, I ended up receiving much more than what I had given.

It happened when I met with my friend's daughter to help her with the challenges she was facing in her life. The daughter had an executive job at the bank with great success but in her personal life, her relationship was going sour. The daughter was happy to meet with me and we went for coffee to see if I could be of any help.

After two hours of stories and discussions, my friend's daughter stood up and said "Edna, I've decided you are going to be a coach!" I just looked at her with astonishment and didn't know exactly what to say. She added that she had a life coach at the bank, and since she works as a professional human resources officer, she knows to identify strengths in people. She could see that I had the qualities of a coach.

It took me completely by surprise. Even though I always helped people in their finances and in different challenges of life, I never thought about becoming a coach. In return for my willingness to help, I received a new mission and career, which is what I am currently doing, empowering women as a coach and a mentor.

Opportunities are disguised and they appear when they are the least expected. Open your heart to different opportunities; you never know which door will open for you and what opportunity you will find behind the door.

ONLY A SMILE

She was on her way to the shop to buy bread, eggs, and milk. On the way, she smiled at a stranger she met who looked sad. It appeared like the smile made him feel better. He remembered his friend that helped him a while ago, and when he arrived home he decided to write a thank you letter to his friend.

The friend was so happy when he got the thank you letter that on the very same evening, he left a big tip for the waitress in the restaurant where he had dinner with his wife.

The waitress, surprised and excited from the tip she got, gave some of it to a beggar who was sitting in the street corner on her way home.

The beggar was very thankful, since for the last two days he was sad and lonely and he didn't have much to eat. After finishing the dinner he bought with the money the waitress had given him, he went to his old and dirty room to sleep.

On the way he found an old dog, which was lonely and dirty. He took the dog to his room to give him some shelter from the cold and the rain.

That night, a fire broke out in his building that threatened to burn the whole building down.
The dog woke up and started barking until the beggar and all of the neighbors in his building had woken up. The dog saved them all.

One of the neighbors was the same girl that smiled with a look full of warmth to the stranger she met the previous day.

The world goes round and round, and whatever you send out, you'll get back in return. We are all connected in one-way or another.

If you are looking for love, be a loving person and give love to others.
If you want more smiles, smile to others generously, and you may never know the effect of your smile on another person. Give yourself permission to try it.

➢ Embrace new opportunities

➢ Open your heart to different opportunities

➢ Enjoy every opportunity

"Women have expectations that they can have and do everything. Once they realize that they can't have it all, they are left with the feeling of not good enough. Find your heart, listen to your heart and follow your heart!"

Lisa - In 2 Balance Kinesiology
www.in2balancekinesiology.com.au

May your choices reflect Your HOPES Not your fears.

Nelson Mandela

Chapter 2

The Power to Change

2.1   The Power to Change

We all have the power to change.

There are many times in our lives when we have succumbed to our faith. We think that whatever happens to us *is what it is*. We don't even think about changing it. We are not sure how to change, we are scared to make a move, we might think, "It's too difficult," "I don't want to rock the boat," "if I will change, I will not be me," or any other thought that stops us from making a decision to change.

Change is all around us. If you look at the weather, it is forever changing; the sun or moon's position, the wind, and the clouds – they are all in constant move and change.

Technology is another part of life that is changing and evolving continuously. Everything around us is changing, nothing is staying still and the same.

As you have to adapt yourself to the change that occurs around you, think about creating change in your life as part of life, it is also a necessity for growth and development.

We often stay where we are, unable to decide to change. Change is not always easy. And the fear of change is what keeps us in situations that are not to our advantage. Sometimes, courage is all we need to make a change, or we wait until it becomes just unbearable.

Sometimes you might wait and hope that things will change. You might hope that people will change, that situations and outcomes will change, but from life experiences we know that "hope" is not a strategy. Just by hoping, things usually don't change.

To some people, to make a change is not always easy, but you need to consider the alternative, the other option, which is to stay in the same state. The situation you wish to change is not always a comfortable one, an easy one, the one that you really want, or the one that makes your life the way you desire. Think and imagine the change you can create and the improvement you will achieve in your life.

There is another way, a way to decide that you want change in your life and *take action*.

- If something is not working well – *change it.*
- If a relationship is not how you want it – *change it.*

  When a key is not opening the door easily, we replace it and buy a new key.

  In life, it's not always easy but...
- If you want your life to look different – *change it.*
- If you want your life to be a better one – *change it.*

Only YOU have the power to change!

All you need is
courage, *determination* and *action.*

It's not always easy, but it is *possible*!

It's up to **you!**

In which area of your life do you want or need change?

Areas of change can be: work, relationships, health, profession, hobbies, etc.

It all starts with a thought, a thought that something is not working the way it should or the way you want it to be. This thought is then followed by the thought that you want change.

You are the only one in control of your thoughts and the only one that can create change in your life.

Once you make a decision to create change in whatever area of your life, you need to LET GO! You have to let go of the old situation that did not serve you. You have to decide to let it go and actually let it go.

Let It Go

Exercise

Close your eyes and *imagine* that the old situation, relationship, thoughts, or beliefs that are not serving you are packed up in a package, wrapped in an old piece of paper and tied with a rope. Tie a bunch of balloons to this package and take it to the park, to an open space in the park.

Imagine you are holding this package to which a bunch of different colored balloons are tied. You are standing there, in the middle of a grassy area, holding it and preparing yourself to let it go.

Look at it, and when you feel that you are ready to let it go, open your arms and let it go. Look at the package going up towards the beautiful blue sky. You can see it moving from side to side as it goes up and becoming smaller and smaller and fading away.

Watch it slowly disappear into the bright sun and notice how it becomes smaller and smaller. Now you see it as a far away dot until it disappears.

Your old problem has just disappeared.

In the parcel were your old situations, thoughts or beliefs. Once you let them go, replace them with the thoughts or situations you would like to invite into your life.

❖ What would you like to invite into your life now?

❖ Write it down and create your new reality.

❖ Believe in yourself – you can do it!

- ➤ Only YOU have the power to change
- ➤ Only YOU have the power to create change in your life
- ➤ Hope is not a strategy
- ➤ Choose the life that you wish for yourself

The change starts with
You!

2.2 Change Your Story –
Change Your Life

Everyone has a story. People often will tell their story. Some of these stories are incidents that happened in their lives.

Most of the time, events that have happened to us, especially in our childhood, leave us with faded memories and conclusions that we had made at that time, based on our feelings then.

Those conclusions are emotional conclusions that we carry with us for many years or for the rest of our lives.

Some build their life story upon those memories and emotions, life stories that are not always factual or true. But we live our lives believing those stories, as they become part of us.

Some of the conclusions of those stories we carry with us are very simple, but their effect on our lives is profound. Our conclusions can be:

- I am stupid
- I am not clever
- I am too slow
- I am too fat
- I can't study
- I am too strong
- I am too weak
- I am too old
- I am too smart
- I am not good enough

And the list goes on and on.

It is "your story," **but** *it's not always the truth!*

It's just a story! It's just what you say about yourself; it's a made-up story, and you believe in it. Your story does not serve you, and it will not set you free.

You are confusing yourself with your story. *You,* are not your story!

You can let go of your story, the story that doesn't serve you anymore. You are invited to do a personal check up and find out if you have a story that is ruling your life.

Answer the following questions:

- What is *your story*?
- Which story has been affecting your life?
- For how long have you believed in your story?
- How would your life be without your story?
- Does your story serve you?
- If not...

**Are you prepared to give it up?
To let it go?**

If your answer is **"YES,"** you can use the *Let Go exercise* (see page 40).

You can also consider answering the following questions:

- How can you take this story and convert it to something great?
- Can you take your story and replace it with a new one?

Once you *let go* of your "story," *decide* which success story will you replace it with.

Now that you don't have the heavy burden of your story, who will you be?

You have a large variety of choices; you can be or do anything your heart desires.

Choose carefully and enjoy your choice.

Personal trainers, coaches, and consultants are hired to inspire people to achieve things they did not believe they could achieve to begin with. They do not listen to "your story," of what you can or can't achieve. In fact, they are working with your potential, for you to achieve beyond your expectations.

When I coach people, it's my job to connect them to who they really are. Often, I point at the sky and indicate that the sky is their limit. My aim is to get them to their source of pure joy of action inside them, which is the source of power to achieve.

It was a beautiful clear day when the two young brothers went for a walk in Antarctica.
The two brothers enjoyed the nice weather and the views along the frozen lake. Suddenly one of the children stepped on thin ice and fell into the freezing water.

His brother was distraught and didn't waste any time. He jumped into the frozen water and helped his brother get out. Their parents arrived within minutes. They were worried and upset and they hardly could believe their children's story.

49

How can such a small child jump into the freezing water without drowning?

An old man approached the parents and told them, "I know how your child saved his brother". "How?" the father asked.

The old man came closer to the father and said: "There was no one there to tell him that he couldn't do it!" smiling, quietly he left the area.

It doesn't matter what's been written in your story so far, it's how you fill up the rest of the pages that count.

➢ What is your story?

➢ Does it serve you?

➢ Let go of your story

➢ Create your new story

➢ Yes! You can

"Just do it! Don't be afraid to fail. Just be brave,
allow yourself to be brave, have courage! Keep on...
give yourself permission to be brave."

Brook Squires –Raw Africa Eco Tours
www.rawafricaedotours.com

----

*Impossible is only
an opinion*

NOT a fact

2.3   Heal Your Soul –

Eliminate Illness

As it happens in my life, I was introduced to Recall Healing a while ago. While viewing some videos that I was given to watch to check their content, some old knowledge emerged that was very interesting, and new to me. It made a lot of sense, and it was an enjoyment to learn.

This was another suggestion I received – I call it "a gift" – to specialize in Recall Healing, which I embraced, and has added a new dimension to my coaching.

I started to enquire and learn further about Recall Healing until I found myself in a course that taught how to use it to prevent illnesses and heal others. I am now practicing Recall Healing with great results that heal a wide variety of illnesses.

Recall Healing is based on the theory that all our diseases are triggered by an emotional conflict. Recall Healing works to identify and resolve the emotional trauma behind the condition, which contributes to the healing process.

Instantaneous healing takes place when the conflict underlying the illness is resolved by new awareness.

I often emphasize the importance of loving yourself, letting go of life stories that are stealing your livelihood, and forgiving the people who have created hurt, pain and unhappiness in your life.

I would like to add how important it is to forgive and let go, since those traumas and emotional conflicts, in time, create havoc and *dis-ease* in our bodies that translate to disease and illness. The benefit of letting go is yours to enjoy!

When you carry the burden of pain, emotional agony, and hurt, you are binding yourself to the past and your body is aching and suffering. Forgiveness and release of past pains cures more illnesses than any antibiotics.

One of my clients came to me with a rare form of disease in her lungs. She was unable to breath, on very strong medications, and was unable to work or live a normal life. She was breathing with great difficulty and was crying often.
In a very short time, we identified the underlying issue that stole oxygen from her lungs and her life. We discovered that the difficult and upsetting relationships she had with close family members was the culprit stealing her breath and her livelihood.

Once we identified the trigger, and with helpful tools of how to let go and forgive, the lungs healed in no time at all. The symptoms disappeared, and now, whenever I talk to her, I am greeted with the biggest smile possible.

Live in the present; don't drag your past into your present or your future.

Release your pain and hurt, and live a healthy fruitful life.

- ➤ Eliminate illness heal your soul
- ➤ Let go and forgive those who hurt you
- ➤ Forgiveness and release of past pain cures better than antibiotics
- ➤ Release your pain and live a happy healthy life

*"Embrace change in small steps,
accept the change with the notion of
"I can do it!" See the change as positive and
permanent."*

Naras Lapsys – The Body Doctor
www.thebodydoctor.com.au

You have the power,
The power is within you!

2.4 Embrace Change

You often hear about people that don't like change. Some people are very scared of change. Many people would have loved to change their circumstances, to have better or easier situations, but they don't like to make the change. They don't have the courage to initiate change. They are scared to take charge and to take the first steps. They are scared of the unknown, since they don't know what the results of their actions will be. They are afraid to get lost in a new territory.

One has to *want* change in order to change. No one can change without the will to do it, and no one can do it for you.

People usually are resistant to change. They are safe where they are. They know that to rock the boat is easy, but to fight the waves, and not being sure how high they will be, will be an entirely new challenge.

Change is a process:

The first stage of change is awareness; it's an understanding and the acceptance that you are not in the right place or situation.

Once awareness sets in, you have to eliminate your resistance. Most people are resistant to change. You have to know how to avoid resistance and increase your desire to be in a better place.

Resistance comes from a place of fear, as we resist in order to protect what we have now, what we know now and what we experience now.

For some, change is very scary so they resist anything that will make them move to uncharted waters.

To avoid resistance, the first step is to be open to new ideas, new options, new possibilities, and to be receptive to accept that there are new and sometimes different ideas, opinions and options.

You have to be aware of new possibilities and sometimes new knowledge, to be open to listen and maybe to learn something new.

The most important thing to avoid resistance is to acknowledge your fear and decide to be courageous and try new things. Give a chance to new possibilities.

The next step is to accept change.
You have to recognize the situation that you are in, and accept that change is the only and the best option to achieve a better outcome, to give you a better life.

You have to take responsibility and acknowledge where you are now and what change you would like to achieve.

When you have the awareness without resistance, you can recognize the situation and take responsibility. Only then you can achieve the change you wish to embrace.

Change is *not* always easy, and sometimes you need some outside help of a friend or a coach. As a coach, I often describe my help resembling a surf lifesaver, which is trained to save a person that is trapped in a whirlpool and can't see a way out. All this person needs is someone to extend an arm to them and to pull them out of the water. I call it "A helping hand."

I am a big believer of change. I believe that every change is usually a good change. Even if one thinks change may lead to a bad situation, one never knows the long-term outcome, as the roads of life sometimes have their own ways of bringing us to a better outcome.

Even a small change, like cleaning and clearing your wardrobe, allows for new space and for new items to be added to your wardrobe.

When I coach, I often get to engage in conversations about change and the opportunities that change provides. I love to share my personal stories as clients find them interesting and enriching examples.

When my marriage and my partnership in the business ended, many of my family members and friends were extremely upset about it. This followed by selling my part of the business, and leaving the business I co-built and managed, which had been the center of my life. Nothing in my life felt easy.

But I was very calm. Somehow, I started to believe in change, and that change is a good thing and I saw it as a situation where new doors will open for me.

Following the separation, instead of being involved in the business and spending long days in the office without much time for myself or my hobbies, I found myself at the beginning of a "new space," a space where I had "nothing special" to do. To some people, this might sound a bit frightening, since the "new space" might seem like a void, but very quickly I found new and interesting activities to fill up my days.

I found an exercise class to keep me in shape. I went to different seminars to enrich my knowledge, like Real Estate Investments and Internet Marketing, which I started engaging in. I learned to be a coach and helped many women succeed in their professional and personal lives.

I became more involved in my community and was appointed as the president of my community's club. I started painting, which I longed to do for many years, but had no time for before, as I was too tired after a day's work at the office. And the most important change was that suddenly I had some spare time for myself, to enjoy it the way I wanted to.

I wouldn't have done all those new and enjoyable activities if I would have stayed and continued working in the business.

With change you create new possibilities. New options appear, possibilities, which you wouldn't and couldn't have seen before.

If you want a different outcome to a current situation, embrace change. Sometimes *courage* is needed to create something new and unknown, but if you believe that everything will turn out for the better, that is what will happen.

- Develop awareness for change
- Eliminate resistance to change
- Take responsibility to create change
- With change come new possibilities
- Embrace change
- Be kind to yourself
- If you never try, you'll never know

When life gives you lemons,
Make lemonade!

2.5 Predict Your Future

Is it possible to predict your future?
Yes, it is!

The best way to predict your future is to *create* it. But how do you create the future, you might ask?

Well, it's easier than you think. Yes, you can predict your future - not all of it, but you can control some parts of your future. You have the control to choose what to study, your partner, friends, your profession, work place, a hobby and much more. We have many choices in life, but we do not always pay attention to the choices we have in front of us.

Surely we also have life events that are not under our control, but when we are in a situation where we can choose and we know what we want, we have to know how to make it happen.

I recall many years ago, I helped a friend that wanted to buy an apartment and didn't know how to approach it.

I suggested she writes on piece of paper a list of exactly what she wanted: the size of the apartment, how many bedrooms, the location, what she wanted to have in her new apartment, and the price she was prepared to pay for it.

It took her a bit of time and some thinking to complete the list. You are not always aware of all the details of what you really want, and you don't always think about all the specific details, until you make a list.

Her list comprised of:

A house in a specific suburb
A house in a very good condition
3 bedrooms with built-ins
2 bathrooms
Laundry with room for the washing machine and dryer
A nice kitchen
A good size garage
A small garden
A specific price $$$$$
Bought by _____ (a certain date)

With her finished list, my friend couldn't believe how clear the picture of the apartment she wanted appeared to her now.

She was now clear about what she wanted and was prepared to convey to the agents what exactly she wished for. In no time, she found an apartment, and she was very surprised to find one that ticked all of the boxes of her desires.

Be open getting exactly what you want, or at least very close to what you want.

For many years I've been using this method, years before I became a coach. I was very surprised to study about it as part of my coaching course. Now when I coach, I teach others how to achieve their goals. It is a very simple method that proves itself time after time.

Your goals can be about getting a new job, planning a holiday, purchasing a new home, starting a new business, participating in a new course, saving money for a special project, or any other goal you may have.

Decide which goal you would like to achieve and
Create your goal:

1. Make a list of all the details of your goal.
2. Choose the 10 most important items.
3. Prioritize them: from 1-10 where number 1 is the most important one.
4. Set the price/value in $.
5. Decide the achievement date.
6. Describe your goal in one sentence.
7. Write it as a headline in a newspaper.
8. Read it aloud and check if it is exactly the goal you want, including the due date.
9. Make it exciting and challenging, a description that when you read it, puts a smile on your face.

Take your time to make your list. Include in it all the details you want to achieve. Once it is ready, write it on a nice piece of paper and place it where you can see it often.

Follow your list and start to take action. The list alone will not create your outcome. Take the right steps to see the goal coming to life.

Celebrate every goal that you achieve –
you deserve it!

- ➢ Create your future
- ➢ Set your goals
- ➢ Write down your goals
- ➢ List the details of each goal
- ➢ Set stepping stones to achieve them
- ➢ Go for it!

The best way to predict
your future
Is
To create it

Chapter 3

Your Authentic "You"

3.1 Your Authentic Voice

When talking to women, the following subjects appear very slowly: confidence, honesty, and authentic communication. Without these traits, people don't experience an honest and enjoyable life where they can communicate their truth in an easy and pleasant way.

What is an authentic voice?

Are you using your authentic voice?

Your authentic voice is the voice you use to participate in conversations and to share whatever is on your mind: "I don't agree" or "Yes, I agree." Express your opinions, articulate your emotions, and just speak your truth.

Many times we don't enter conversations because we don't think we can say what we really want. We sell ourselves short. We quit before we even have a chance to succeed.

You have to trust your authentic voice and your ability to communicate with your family, friends, co-workers and supervisors at work, and others with authenticity and clarity.

Over the years in my career as a coach, I realized that many people just couldn't communicate their truth. Sometimes, the reason is that in a past experience, something happened to them.
Possibly, in their childhood, someone told them that what they said was trivial, or they had an incident where other students in their class laughed at them when they said something that didn't sound right. Maybe one of their parents didn't have the patience to listen to them, ignored them, or just told them "that's silly," "don't be silly," or "that's not right."

That might have caused them to arrive to the conclusion: "I am dumb," "I am stupid, so I should say very little," "I should say only what the other person likes to hear," or "I should follow others since I am not clever." In those moments, a decision was made to hide their own truth and their authentic voice.

While coaching and helping women find their own authentic voice and live an authentic life, seeing the change it created in their lives and in the lives of others around them, I understood how important it is to use your Authentic Voice and what a difference it can create in one's life.

I remember when I was about fifteen years old, I went to my neighbor, a guy that was four years older than me, to ask for a book. We started to chat and we got to the subject of boyfriends, girlfriends, and relationships.

As I was younger than him, my neighbor started advising me about etiquette with boys: how to dance with them, where to put my arms around them, etc. He continued his advice with a special point - he told me that he wants to give me a piece of advice that is very important and that I should always remember.

As I never had a boyfriend before, I was very tuned in to what he had to say. His advice was that I should ALWAYS be very HONEST and AUTHENTIC with any boyfriend that I have. I should tell him exactly what I think and what I feel, to eliminate any misunderstandings and to keep a strong and honest relationship.

As I was young, with no experience in this area, I nodded and agreed to keep this promise. I didn't realize then how important his advice was. I lived all my life with this promise at the back of my mind, and only years later, I realized how it shaped my life and what a great advice it was.

In order to have an authentic life, use your authentic voice. Talk to others with authenticity, say and express exactly whatever is on your mind without fear or doubt.

Trust your authentic voice and live a life where you can express your wants, wishes, and feelings with peace.

To start the journey of living with an authentic voice in order to have good communication with others, we should first communicate with authenticity with ourselves.

You might ask, what do you mean to live with an authentic voice?

In order to live with an authentic voice, imagine yourself:

- Communicating with your spouse, parents, kids, friends, or people at work with full honesty.

- Saying what you really think and feel authentically.

- Managing any conversation with honesty and calmness.

- Expressing your honest feelings whenever you want and need.

- Expressing your honest feelings with calmness and ease.

- Solving any conflict with ease and peace.

- Living your life authentically every day with ease and joy.

The results of honest and authentic communication will translate to spending your time and energy enjoying your relationships with everyone in an honest, easy, and enjoyable way.

Finding your authentic voice will set you on a path so that you can really be yourself and **SHINE!**

➢ Use your authentic voice

➢ Communicate with honesty and calmness

➢ Enjoy honest relationships with everyone

"You cannot heal what you refuse to confront, search within yourself, know yourself."

Kerri – Amorah Kinesiology
www.amorahkinesiology.com.au

Be yourself,
Let your unique qualities
SHINE!

3.2 Use Your Authentic Voice

In order to enjoy our lives, we have to speak and communicate with everyone with an authentic voice. With everyone, I mean: your life partner, parents, children, family, and friends, at work and at home - everyone you interact with.

Do you have an authentic voice?

To enjoy an authentic life, you need to communicate your feelings and thoughts in an honest way: to say exactly what you think and what you feel. You want to communicate and convey your thoughts in a clear and honest way, so others will understand you in order to eliminate misunderstandings and confusion.

Are you using your authentic voice?

Sometimes you listen to people speak and you can feel that they are hiding some details or they are avoiding telling the whole story. It leaves you feeling uneasy and with feelings of dishonesty and deceit.

When we talk to people, sometimes we can omit some parts of the story or change some details in order to justify ourselves.

We do it in order to be accepted, to look good or to modify our story to whatever we want to convey. In those situations, we are not using our authentic voice. Using your authentic voice is to share and express your opinions with honesty and ease, to articulate your emotions with authenticity or, in short, to speak your truth.

Is your authentic voice hiding?
Where can you find it?

In order to have simple, easy and joyful relationships with others, you have to communicate with honesty. You have to say what you think and feel. Things are much simpler when the other person knows exactly what you mean. Though, it's not always easy. At times, when you are in a difficult situation, when telling the truth is uncomfortable and/or for the other person to hear, you have to find a way to convey the message, even if it's not a pleasant one.

Many years ago, when I did a big party for a family celebration, I couldn't include all my friends and acquaintances. I was restricted in the number of people I could invite, and I couldn't include all the people I wanted to include.

It was an unpleasant situation for me especially since some of the people were expecting to be invited. I thought about it a lot and I didn't feel good about upsetting the people I couldn't invite (no matter how much I wanted to).

After debating about it for a while, I decided to let the people that I couldn't invite know my situation ahead of time. It wasn't an easy decision, but I knew that it would eliminate many disappointments, misunderstandings, and quarrels.

I called those people and explained my situation. I told them how I really wanted to invite them, that they are important to me, and that I was limited in the number of people I could invite. I told them that I appreciate their friendship and that I am very sorry I couldn't invite them but am hopeful we will meet soon in other happy occasions.

To my surprise, all of the people I talked to expressed their understanding of the situation and wished me well.

I have to admit that it wasn't easy and these were not the most enjoyable conversations, but everyone understood the difficult position I was in.

When you convey your thoughts and emotions in an honest way, people immediately feel it and support you. You always have to convey your thoughts authentically. Explain your position and the situation you are in so others understand you.

Imagine how many misunderstandings you can avoid with an authentic conversation.

Imagine living a peaceful life with your life partner - living a life where everything is discussed and agreed upon with honesty and peace. Imagine having an understanding of situations where you don't have to stress about them or guess what the other person is thinking.

Picture yourself at work, where your relationships with your superiors and colleagues are honest and easy. Where you can convey your thoughts, plans and intentions in an authentic way so no one has to guess, assume or speculate about what you mean or what will happen.

This changes your whole environment. Your surroundings become happy and friendly.

Imagine no more disappointments and no more unknown expectations. Everything becomes calm, relaxed, and stress-free.

Once you realize how easy it can be to use your authentic voice, you'll enjoy a much more peaceful and fulfilled life. When you change your behaviour, the behavior of others around you changes, too. Observe how the reaction of others around you changes in response to your authenticity - you'll be surprised.

When you try it, you'll see your life changing to a more joyful one.

- ➤ Are you using your authentic voice?
- ➤ Live an authentic life with ease and joy
- ➤ Live your life powerfully

Use your authentic voice
And live your life
Powerfully

3.3 Live Your Truth

It is very important to use your authentic voice - that is, to say exactly what you think. But it is another matter to *live* your truth.

To live your truth is about living in a way that suits you - in other words, to do what you really want to do. So many people, especially women, live according to other people's standards and wishes. It might be a parent, partner, husband, wife, or any other person that has power over you or that you have given your power to.

Choose the way you really want to live. Choose the life you wish, deserve, and desire. Don't give other people the power to decide how to live your life. Your life belongs to YOU!

Live authentically all day, every day, with everyone and in every area of your life. Live authentically with your partner, family members, friends, work colleagues, and especially your children. It won't always be comfortable, but life is easier when you are honest with others about your thoughts, wishes, and actions.

Explain your thoughts and actions to clarify why you do things the way you do them. Sometimes others understand your thoughts and actions differently. When you clarify them, there is less disappointment and more understanding and appreciation.

Keeping your thoughts to yourself will only build barriers in your relationships, as others will always translate your actions into their own language – they will translate them according to their own thoughts, actions, and experiences. Others do not always think the same way as you do; they just translate things to their own perspective.

Deliver your truth; when you think about something, say it the way you believe it. Say exactly what you want, wish, or desire for yourself without taking any shortcuts. Your life belongs to you, and you should be the one to decide how to live it.

Plan your life and live the life you want. Trust your truth, as it is Your Truth.

- ➢ Live your truth
- ➢ Clarify your thoughts and actions
- ➢ Trust your truth

You are the CEO of
your own life

And you have to make all
Your decisions

Chapter 4

Permission to Want More

4.1 Permission to Want...More

Most women believe that they have to put everyone else first, putting their needs and aspirations last in their list of concerns. Mothers tend to have the responsibility to look after their families, and they often forget to think and care about themselves. They just forget about their own needs and aspirations since they have to make sure that their family is looked after.

You might recall my previous statement, to "Treat Yourself as Gold," but I would like to extend it and take it or two steps further.

As women, most of us are looking after our immediate family and sometimes after our extended family too, such as our parents or other relatives.

We forget that we have PERMISSION TO WANT! We have permission to dream and to aspire for different things in our lives. We don't have to wait for anyone to give us permission or to ask permission from anyone, we only have to give ourselves the permission to want.

Give yourself the permission to want, open your arms and recognize that you also have the permission to want MORE!

Sometimes due to limited finances, obligations and responsibilities, we do not think we have time nor space to think about ourselves. And for other women, it's just not in their awareness to attend to their needs or dreams.

To some, to think about their wants, needs and desires might sound odd and unrealistic, as it is not in their awareness to think about it. They are too involved with their everyday lives to think about themselves.

Once you bring your desires into your awareness it can become a reality. Maybe it won't happen straight away, sometimes it's just not the right time, but your awareness will keep your plan or your dream alive for you and it will eventuate in it's own good time.

For many women, this realization might come naturally only later in life, when their kids are getting older or grown up. At this point, they might find more time for themselves to think about their lives and what else they would like to do or achieve.

Sometimes they come to this realization when they are older and suddenly realize that there is more to life and then start thinking about themselves.

You don't have to wait to get to a certain situation or age to think about your own needs and aspirations. You can consider them at any age and make them happen.

What do *you want* and you never *dared to ask*?

What do *you need* and you never *dared to ask*?

What would you like *to achieve* and you never *dared to think* about?

Exercise:

One option is to add your dreams and aspirations to your to-do list and know that you have permission not only to want but also to *want more* in your life. If you don't have a to-do-list, now is the time to create one.

When you add your wants, dreams and aspirations to your to-do list, add an achievement date. The date in your to-do list can be for today, tomorrow or a few years down the line.

It will be your reminder to reach your goals by a certain time. If you leave it without a date, it will stay only as a wish.

Write it down so it will stay somewhere in your mind and it won't disappear, getting in the mix of all your everyday activities and responsibilities.

To get your goals on the path to achieve them, plan the stepping-stones that will get you to them.

Be generous and think about the things you would like to achieve in a big way.

Don't be afraid to dream big. Give yourself the permission to **DREAM BIG!**

At one of my seminars "Goals4Success," one of the participants was telling us that she doesn't have any special goals at the present time and that the only goal she has is to sell her business in about five years.

I suggested to her to write her goals for selling her business and to date them - forecasting when and how she would like it to transpire. I also explained that long-term goals are setting up in our subconscious and eventuate in time.

She agreed to my suggestions and created her goals for five years in the future.

The years have passed and, as life went by, she forgot about the seminar she enjoyed and the goals she had set.

One day I heard that she had sold the business so I called to congratulate her. She was very excited and told me all about the buyer and the sale of the business with the agreement to continue to work in the business for another six months, transferring the business at the end of that period.

I was very happy for her - it was her life project and selling the business enabled her to make life changes and start a new chapter in her life.

Later that day, I was thinking how happy she was of the sale of the business and a thought came to my mind, I remembered that her goal at my seminar was to sell the business and it was set for five years in the future. I went to check my notes, to verify the seminar's date. To my surprise it was exactly five years earlier.

With the experience of assisting many people in setting their goals, I know that if a goal is set properly, most likely it will eventuate. But still, to see it happening was exciting for me. When you don't expect something, it appears as an exceptional delight.

Allow yourself to dream and give yourself permission not only to want, but also to want more.

- ➤ Identify your wants, wishes, and aspirations
- ➤ Give yourself permission to want
- ➤ Give yourself permission to want more
- ➤ Set goals to achieve
- ➤ Write your goal down and set an achievement date
- ➤ Set the stepping stones to achieve your goals

The difference between
Ordinary and Extraordinary
life
is that
Little "extra"!

4.2 Respect Your Feelings

We all have feelings - feelings of happiness, sadness, generosity, desire, loneliness, love, anger, frustration, and many other feelings. Sometimes we can feel our feelings as butterflies in our stomach, and at other times we can feel them as anger climbing to our face.

Some people are aware of their feelings and others stay oblivious to them. Others are aware that sometimes they have feelings of jealousy, anger, love, or others, but they don't listen to those feelings. They are not attuned to them.

I believe that our feelings were created as a sign for us to notice and observe them. They are a way for our body, mind, and soul to notify us about our state of mind. Don't disregard them. Follow and listen to your feelings.

I learned from an early age to be attuned and listen to my feelings, Over the years, I came to the realization that whenever certain feelings surfaced, they were always accurate; they were signaling the truth for me.

I learned *not to doubt them* and, on the contrary, listen to them. As I always say **"My feelings never lie."**

At times in my previous career, I would meet with directors or export managers of multinational spare parts companies. At those meetings, I was listening, watching, and observing people talk.

I remember very clearly at the end of some meetings, I was telling my team, "Did you see that person telling us what we wanted to hear instead of the truth?" or "Did you notice how that person was misleading us in a big way!"

My team sometimes looked at me and asked "But how do you know? How did you see it?" And my reply was always, "It was written on his forehead - didn't you see it?" They would look at me with surprise and with big open eyes as if asking: how did it happen that you saw it and we didn't?

Just by observing people talk and the way they conduct themselves you can see many things. If you really listen to others without letting your mind wander or thinking about what to say next, you can identify and understand many things that are said and especially things that are not said.

Over time, my feelings were proven to be true, and in business they were used as a tool. I think that all this observation started when I was a young girl, sitting quietly and just listening to people's conversations and observing them. I was watching them talk and observing their behavior.

You can develop those qualities too: listen and observe, be aware and pay attention. Pay attention to how people talk, choose their words, and react and especially notice their body language. You have to be attuned, and in no time, you'll develop awareness.

Our body reacts to what we say and what is said to us. Our body feels it, too. But we are not conscious or sensitive enough to those signs.

Sometimes we are too involved in listening to a person, telling us exactly what we want to hear but not telling us the truth, but just by looking at that person and being aware and listen to our body's reaction, we can feel if it's true or false.

Listen to your feelings:

- If you are told to do something and you don't have a good feeling about it – **don't do it**
- If you want to buy something and you have doubts about it – **don't buy it**
- If you have to go somewhere and you don't feel good about it – **don't go**
- If you have to do something and you are too scared – **don't do it**
- If you have to meet people that you dislike and you feel the resentment – **don't meet them**

Listen to your body and to your feelings, they know best!

100

Feelings are everywhere as in
"The Folly of Love":

Somewhere in the world, all the feelings gathered for a special meeting. At the meeting they were bored, and *Craziness* got up and said, "Let's play hide-and-seek!"

Curiosity, who was always impatient, asked, "How do you play hide-and-seek?"

Craziness explained, "I will cover my eyes, count to one thousand, you will all hide, and at the end of my counting, I will look for you."

Excitement danced with *Euphoria. Happiness* jumped ever so high, which convinced *Doubt* and Indifference to join in.

But not everyone really wanted to join in.

Truth preferred not to hide since she believed that she would be exposed at the end, anyway.

Pride said that the game was silly. (What really bothered her was the fact that the idea wasn't hers.)
"One... two... three" *Craziness* started to count.

The first one to hide was *Laziness*, who hid under the first rock she could find. *Jealousy* went to hide in the shadow of *Success*; with great effort she found a spot on top of the tallest tree.

Generosity could hardly hide since every spot she found looked to her a better place for one of her friends: "A hole in a tree trunk was perfect for *Modesty*, and behind the butterfly wings was perfect for *Sensuality*," she thought.

Finally she found the right place for herself in a small ray of sunshine.

Desire found a place inside a volcano, and *Love* found a great space in a bush of roses.

"One thousand!" Counted *Craziness*, and he started his search.

First to be found was *Laziness*, just three steps away.

Doubt was found next, sitting on a fence, still debating where to hide.

Then they heard *Desire*, shaking the volcano.
Suddenly *Jealousy* appeared, and that was how *Success* was found.

Only *Love* could not be found.

Craziness looked under each stone, behind every tree, and on top of each hill.

Just about to give up, he saw the bushes of roses and started searching between the branches.

Unexpectedly, a scream was heard. It was *Love*; the thorns wounded her eyes.

Craziness was so upset; he apologized and cried, begged for forgiveness, and even promised to follow *Love* wherever she goes.

And ever since that day, *Love* is blind and *Craziness* comes with her.

- ➢ Respect your feelings
- ➢ Listen to your feelings
- ➢ Trust your feelings
- ➢ Your feelings never lie

*"Never underestimate your intuition
and listen to your gut feeling.
Follow your passion is a powerful thing."*

Nic – PH Clinic - Colonic Hydrotherapy
www.phclinic.com.au

Follow your feelings
Your feelings never lie
Your feelings have no agenda!

4.3 Respect Your Needs

We all have needs - some have more and some have less. As women, we often neglect to recognize or think about our needs. Some of our needs are to love, be loved, get attention, be creative, be looked after, continue learning, have special time for ourselves, time for friends or shopping, increase our personal development, develop new hobbies, take on further education, doing sport, or any other need for our wellbeing.

- What are your needs?

- What are the things you would like to have achieved or to enjoy that are not fulfilled?

- Are your needs important to you?

- Do you have any free time for your needs? Or do you always think about others?

- Do you tell yourself "There are other people or other things more important than me; therefore I don't need it"?

- What priority do you give yourself? Are you first priority or last?

- Or do you think that you don't deserve to have any needs?

These are important questions to ask yourself; they can bring your needs to the surface.

Respect yourself and your needs since they will make you a happier person - a satisfied and fulfilled one so you can attend to the needs of other family members with joy and patience.

When you create a list of your goals, remember to include your needs. Write them on top of your list, as a priority.

No one can tell you or decide for you what your needs are, you are the only one that knows exactly what they are.

You are special; you *deserve* to have your needs fulfilled!

Respect your needs for a better future for yourself and your family. It's not only you that will enjoy your fulfilled needs. When you are happy and satisfied, everyone around you enjoys you and your input as a daughter, partner, mother, or a friend. You will have so much more to give to others from yourself when you are enriched.

Enjoy your needs; enjoy the feeling of being satisfied and happy.

> ➤ Know your needs
> ➤ Respect your needs
> ➤ Make your needs important
> ➤ You deserve to enjoy your needs

*"Take care of yourself, do things for yourself
to boost your confidence."*

Donna Lee Marcal – Dermatonics
www.dermatonics.com.au

If you could add one more hour
To your day,
How would you spend it?

4.4 Set Your Boundaries

Many houses have fences. Some fences are small, some are tall, and some houses instead have a line of trees or a driveway that shows the boundaries. Fences are built to mark the house boundaries and for protection.

In olden days, many cities in Europe and around the world had high and sturdy walls, built from stones, to protect the city's residents from any conqueror that wanted to capture and occupy the city.

In life, boundaries are like an imaginary fence around your life. They are actually marking your territory. The fence's aim is to keep you safe; it's keeping the unwanted people, events, or behaviors of others out of your life. It keeps your life safe without trespassers, people that can come into your life and treat it as their own or create havoc and damage.

Some people set boundaries (fences) to protect themselves, some build strong and high walls, and some have no boundaries (fences) at all. The ones with *no fences* have not marked their territory and to others it might look like a public place where they can do as they wish.

*You have **NO** boundaries if:*

- People tell you what to do, what not to do or what you should do
- You are criticized often
- You can't say "no"
- You live your life according to other's wishes/expectations
- You are not sure what to do when the advice you are given creates a conflict in you
- You feel that others manage your life
- You are aware that others decide for you
- You can't do what you really want

It is important to know that YOU are the only one in charge of your life!

It's *YOUR life* and you should live it the way you want to.

You should protect your life - protect your territory.

In order to be in charge of your life, you have to set your boundaries. Your boundaries are your fences.
You can decide which fence you would like to build around your life: a small fence, a tall one, or a big wall.
It doesn't matter which boundary you choose.

Boundaries are supposed to be firm walls and not open gates, so it's important to set them up correctly. They should be designed to minimize intrusions and maximize your life's wellbeing.

Choose whom you allow to come through the gate into your territory, who you would allow to advise you, give you their opinions, or share their thoughts. It's up to you! It is okay to put up an imaginary "No Entry" sign for certain people in order to keep your territory safe.

Setting your boundaries is not easy if you have never built them, but it's never too late. Once you set them up, everything around you will change. You will start to be in charge of your life. You will have to decide what you want and what you don't want in your life.

Others will find themselves in a new space, a space where they won't be able to continue to behave as they were used to. They won't understand what happened. Since they won't be able to continue with their old habits and behaviors, they will start to wonder what happened and start to object to the new reality.

Be ready to see them upset, angry, and maybe furious. They will feel that they lost their power. And YOU will have to stay strong in your boots.

You will have to explain that you have decided to be in charge of your life and to live your life the way *you* want, deserve, and dream about.

Be ready for strange and strong reactions from others. *Don't change* your path and *don't compromise* – it is your life that takes first priority.

Once they see you being strong and decisive, they will have no other choice but to let you lead your life the way you choose.

WHEN YOU SET YOUR BOUNDARIES ----- >>>>SHIFT HAPPENS!

➤ *It doesn't suit me*

This is a line that when I explain it to women, and coach them on how to use it, it lights up a light bulb of a new understanding.

Many women never thought of the idea of giving themselves this special and distinct permission, to think about – "Does it suit me? Or maybe, it doesn't suit me." It never crosses their mind to think that way.

As I mentioned before, women usually think about others, everyone else in their family, but they neglect to care for themselves, the way they care for others.

Many times, we do things because we think to ourselves "I have to," "I must do it," or "I have no other choice." It's all about others, never about you. You don't consider your needs, desires and "suitability" into this equation so you don't take into account if it does suit you or it doesn't suit you.

Sometimes you don't want to do things that you are not happy with, enjoy or need to do, or you don't want to do things for any other reason and you don't give it any other thought if it suits you or not.

If you are in doubt about doing or not doing something, talk to certain people, go to certain places or any other situation that you are not sure you would like to be part of, and ask yourself the question "DOES IT SUIT ME?"

TODAY, I would like to give you the permission to think about yourself and to *allow* yourself to ask the question "**Does it suit me**."

When you ask this question, *permit* yourself to **decide**, "It doesn't suit me!"

It is not a selfish decision. It is all about keeping you happy, preserving your boundaries and enjoying your life.

There is no need to tell others that it doesn't suit you. You can decide for yourself that it doesn't suit you and decline doing or taking a part in.

I often hear from my clients, that the question of "Does it suit me," is life changing for them. They enjoy being in control of their lives, decide what suits them and what doesn't suit them. They live an easier life now with added satisfaction and enjoyment.

You are invited to try it and enjoy your life more.

➢ *Is it difficult to say "NO"?*

Boundaries are also about the way you express yourself. As women, we tend to be helpful and caring and at times just respond automatically with a "yes" to many requests. At times, we forget about ourselves and we just say "yes" without paying attention or think twice. And to some of us, it doesn't cross our mind to say anything but "yes".

I come across women who are feeling overloaded, fatigued and especially resentful as they have been put in situations where they've had to do things that they neither want to do, didn't like to do, or didn't have the time to do. It is a reality they create in situations by saying "yes", when actually they should have said "no".
They tend to forget their own needs or have no courage or boundaries to say "no".

They are afraid to look like they are selfish or inconsiderate, but they are actually inconsiderate of their own needs in life. They are anxious about disappointing others. But actually what they do is let themselves down.

Having respect for yourself, your needs, and your life is also a part of your boundaries. Saying "no" when it doesn't suit you is setting your boundaries.

You are **not** selfish or careless; you actually demonstrate to others that you understand *your* limits, *your* priorities, and *your* time, resources, and capabilities.

YES, you are allowed to say "no", "not now" and "no thanks'". When you say "no" with respect, it shows others that you have self-respect and that you have limits.

Learn to say "no" and say it with respect.
Practice it.

As I always say, it's not easy to change your habits, but it is vey possible. You have to be aware of it and do it. At times, you may fall into your old habits, but your awareness will remind you to go back to the new path.

Don't be mean to yourself or beat yourself up if you lose your path. Go back to your new habit, trust yourself that the next time you will remember it.

There is another option instead of saying "no" straight away, and that is to say: "I'll think about it, and I will let you know." This is a great path in order to avoid conflicts and disappointments since the other person is not getting a negative reply and you have the time to think and evaluate your reply. You have your "thinking time" to address the matter. And when you decide about your reply, it is always important to give an explanation, especially when the reply is negative, so that the other person can understand your position.

➢ *Give an explanation*

Explaining your thoughts, feelings, and opinions is also part of your boundaries. It eliminates misunderstandings, frictions, and arguments.

Everyone has his or her own thoughts, and you don't have to think like everyone else. When you explain your position, the other person understands it without giving it his or her own interpretation and it is clear and simple to everyone.

My kids taught me many things, and one of the things they taught me is to give an explanation with my replies to their requests or to my actions. I didn't say: "do this" or "don't do that." I always gave them my explanation first and communicated my line of thought, which followed, by my conclusion.
They understood why I replied the way I did, and it made it logical for them to understand my thoughts and position and accept it.

Try to give explanations as part of your replies. First explain your thoughts and position, so others will understand you and your motives better, and you can avoid misunderstandings and disappointments.

➢ *Just because I can*

At times, we want to do something, but when we think about possible remarks and criticism from our family members, or any other person, we start to apologize for our actions or we stop and just don't do what we wanted.

While observing your boundaries and making your own decisions, the most important thing is to be happy with your decisions, since you are the one responsible for your wellbeing. You can discuss them naturally with whoever you think is suitable or ask for others' opinions, but the decisions should be one hundred percent yours - you have the last word in the matter. You have to feel satisfied and happy with your decisions. As long as you are happy with your decision, that's the most important thing.

Sometimes others question your actions and decisions; some can have different opinions and share their opinions with you. Since the decisions are yours and not theirs, you are the one responsible for them. They are *your* decisions. In those cases I have a saying that I use: "Just because I can." If you have made a decision that others might have an issue with, but you know that you have done the right thing according to your judgement, you can justify it to yourself by saying: "just because I can." As long as you are happy with your choices, that is what counts.

119

➢ *Seal it with a smile*

You are right! When you know that you are right but others criticize you or tell you what you should or shouldn't do, or make an inappropriate remark, don't get into an argument with them. Don't reply in a way that you will be sorry later, don't bring yourself down to their level – just smile!

When you want to reply but you know that the outcome will not be your preferred one or when you want to show another person that you are not joining him or her in their low level behavior – just smile!

A smile is a reply that leaves you with dignity and respect. You let the other person figure out your thoughts. You are sending the other person the message that you are protecting *your* boundaries, *your* self-esteem, and *yourself.* When you get upset and angry because of others' behavior, you join them in their own drama. There is no need to get involved in other people's drama; it is their choice and their life.

Practice smiling and watch their reaction. It is a small gesture that can stop a fight, which would cost you energy, and can instead bring more harmony into your life. Smile to yourself too, and enjoy your inner peace.

- ➢ Set your boundaries
- ➢ Keep them simple
- ➢ Make them important
- ➢ Ask, "Does it suits me?"
- ➢ Practice saying "No"
- ➢ Just because I can
- ➢ Exercise your smiling

"If you want to live longer, you have to exercise. Exercises help your emotional and your mental state. Don't compare yourself to others."

Leilani (Lei) Que – Curves BJ - Curves Bondi Junction
www.curvesbj.com.au

If it cost you your peace
It's too expensive!

4.5 Follow Your Instincts

"My feelings never lie" is a saying that I am always using. Not everyone is attuned to their feelings and instincts. Our body gives us signs, but if we are not accustomed to sensing them or realizing that they are signs from our body, we ignore them.

Our feelings and instincts connect with us in different ways. Some call it a "gut feeling," some call it "intuition," "awareness," or "sensitivity." Those are the feelings that you feel when something feels right or wrong. They are signs that your body and/or your mind are sending you.

Those signs can appear as an understanding - a feeling that all is well, that it is how it should be. It can appear as noises of rumbling in your stomach, a feeling of peace that is spread all over your body, or it can show up in other different ways. Everyone can experience it differently.

On the other hand, when something doesn't feel right, you have a bad feeling that sometimes you can't really explain or you might feel the fear of an undesirable outcome.

You might feel fear, worry, anxiety, unease or even terror. Sometimes they affect you very strongly and they stop you in your tracks and sometimes you are left with feelings of "I am not sure about it."

Once you develop an awareness to listen to your feelings and your instincts, you'll be amazed to see and feel your body's reactions.

Listen when it tells you "yes!" which follows with feelings of happiness and satisfaction or when the feelings appear as worry or fear. Your feelings never lie! Your instincts never lie!

In business and in life, I was always attuned to my instincts and my feelings. At work, at times, I used to say, "I don't have a good feeling about it" and behave according to my feelings.

When I used to interview people for a job, I always was attuned to my feelings during the interview. I was observing the energy the person I interviewed brought with them. I paid attention to my feeling regarding that person after the interview. If I didn't have a good feeling about a certain person, I wouldn't hire them.

I listened to my feelings and followed my instincts. They never lied!

Some of us listen to our feelings and follow our instincts, but others can give logical excuses or explanations and disregard their instincts.

If it's right for you your feelings will react.

And if it's *not* right for you your feelings will react too.

Your awareness is your friend. It is someone that helps you live the life you want. Don't disregard your instincts and feelings, they are your best friends.

➢ Be attuned to your feelings

➢ Listen to your feelings

➢ Follow your instincts

➢ Your feelings never lie!

"Yoga empowers you to notice your body and mind. It gives you tools to focus, notice your breathing and feelings. It inspires you to be your best."

Lindsey – Yoga Village
www.yogavillage.com.au

———————————————

Follow your instincts,
Your instincts never lie!

———————————————

4.6 Never Give Up

As we plan and see our lives emerging, not everything goes according to our plans. We do not always succeed in whatever we plan and work on, and sometimes the disappointments are immense. It's not always our fault, in our control, or in our power to change the outcome. Countless millionaires can tell you about their failure, their losses, bankruptcies, or defeats, but they don't give up.

They also can tell you that the most important ingredients they have, are their courage, determination and positive outlook. They never stumble and stay low on the ground. Instead, they get up, shake the dust off their misfortune, and continue walking with their head held high, confident towards their next adventure, with the confidence that they will succeed.

While I was in business for many years, I watched from a close distance, business owners, friends, and colleagues trying their best in business, investing all their resources, money, efforts, and time in businesses that they believed would be very successful.

They fought long and hard against all different elements that were about to give their business a sudden stop.

Businesspersons have ingrained in them a positive mindset for success, determination, will power, purpose, commitment, drive, and persistence to reach their goals and succeed.

Their biggest mindset is **never give up**!

I remember very clearly a meeting with our accountant many years ago, at the start of our business path.

After checking the figures of our income and expenses for the year, our accountant told us at this meeting that we are just "moving money" – which means that we buy and sell products and after the expenses, nothing is left for us as profit or income.

He said to us that in this position, we could go and get a supplementary income from the government.

We were shocked to hear it from our accountant. We were in business to make money and a good living from it, and we definitely didn't have any inclination or thoughts to ask for government support.

We had a business, we had employees that needed to keep their jobs and livelihood, and we were too proud – we had to do everything in our power to succeed and for sure NOT give up!

This comment didn't depress us; it just made us more determined to put full power into our business and make it work better and more profitable.

To support you to reach YOUR goals and succeed, I invite you to adapt, in every area of your life, a *businessperson's mindset*, a positive mindset that includes *determination*, *will power*, *purpose*, *commitment*, *drive*, and *persistence*, including the businessperson's biggest mindset:

Never give up!

I am including one of my favourite poems that I recount often to demonstrate the meaning and benefit of *"never give up:"*

TWO FROGS IN CREAM

by T.C. Hamlet

Two frogs fell into a can of cream,
Or so I've heard it told;
The sides of the can were shiny & steep,
The cream was deep & cold.
"O, what's the use?" croaked Number One,
"'Tis fate; no help's around.
Goodbye, my friends! Goodbye, sad world!"
And weeping still, he drowned.
But Number Two, of sterner stuff,
Dog-paddled in surprise.
The while he wiped his creamy face
And dried his creamy eyes.
"I'll swim awhile, at least," he said-
Or so I've heard he said;
"It really wouldn't help the world
If one more frog were dead."
An hour or two he kicked & swam,
Not once he stopped to mutter,
But kicked & kicked & swam & kicked,
Then hopped out...
Via butter!

- ➢ Adopt a businessperson's mindset
- ➢ Adopt a positive mindset
- ➢ Adopt determination, willpower and persistence
- ➢ Never give up!

"Always get out of your comfort zone.
Be comfortable to be uncomfortable. Have the
courage to meet your limitations in every single
moment and the will power to step forward and
beyond."

Camila Gayarti – Camila Gayarti Kinesiology
www.camilagayarti.com

What failure are you Grateful for?

Chapter 5

Your Choices

5 Your Choices

Life is full of choices. We all make big and small decisions everyday. Big decisions include choosing our profession, pursuing education, finding a place to live, choosing our friends, partner, husband, or wife. They are the choices that will impact our lives the most.

In everyday life, we have other smaller decisions to make, like: What will you do today? What will you choose to do or not do today?

We all aspire to be something more or something bigger. Sometimes you make the right choices, and sometimes your choices don't work out the way you really want them or planned them.

Your choices shape your life. Your choices really define the way you live your life and the person you are. You and only you have the power to choose what you want your life to look like. It's up to you!

The choice is *YOURS*!

You can choose many things in life. In some areas, your choices can make a big difference and shape your life and add to the quality of your life, like choosing a certain profession that could give you more possibilities, choosing to get married, have a family, or stay single. These are all your choices.

There are other kinds of choices we all can make. I call them the "soft Choices." These choices that can also change, shape, and make a big difference in your life, but they are not always recognized as choices.

They are the elements of life like happiness, confidence, self worth, peace of mind, success, health and many others. Choosing to incorporate these elements into your life can create a better, more enjoyable and satisfying life.

Yes, you might think that it's not always up to you, that you are not always in control of those elements. At first, it might sound a bit odd: Can I choose happiness, success or peace of mind? But once you start thinking about it, you'll find that it's indeed all a matter of choice.

As an example, it's up to you to decide if you want a happy life and decide how to make your life a happy one.

Which elements will you have to exclude from your life in order to have a happy life, and which *happy elements* do you want to invite into your life?

As the CEO of your life, you are the only one that can make the decisions that will shape your life, the life you dream of.

What are your choices?

- ➢ Your "soft choices" are YOUR choices
- ➢ Choose the "soft choices" that will make your life the one you dream of

_____

*Your future depends on many things...
things...
Mostly on
YOU!*

_____

5.1 Choose Happiness

Happiness is a choice.
Happiness is a journey, not a destination.

Invite happiness into your life. In order to invite happiness into your life you have to eliminate doubt, negativity and eliminate all things that are making you angry and upset and eliminate frustrations.

We all have different experiences that create negative emotions in us. It might be someone crossing the road while talking on the phone without noticing their surroundings, a noisy party that interrupts our sleep, a slow driver on the road or any other occurrences at home, at work, or anywhere else. There are many incidents that can cause you to be upset, angry, irritated, or mad. Those are occurrences that you usually have no control over. The only control you have is your *choice* of *reaction*.

When you eliminate your negative emotions and reactions, you can find a way to choose and invite happiness.

Choose happy occasions, happy movies, and happy reactions (like smiling) in order to make your life a happy one. Choose the company of happy people - invite them into your life rather than people who criticize everything and are looking always at things negatively.

Smile often, laugh often; it's good for your body, your mind, and your soul.

Be generous with your smiles. Smile at people in the street, on your walks, or in the shops and see their reactions. Most of them will smile back to you too in return. You might even change someone's day for the better when you smile back to him or her. The effect is *always* positive.

The most important attitude is happiness. Find happiness in whatever you do. Think about people that you meet who are always happy. What are you feeling around them?

Create happiness within yourself; decide to be happy and make your life a happy one. Eventually you will attract other happy people around you and invite others who will enjoy your company and attitude. Happiness is contagious.

Try it; you'll be amazed at the effects.

It would be helpful to ask yourself:

- ✓ Am I choosing happiness today?
- ✓ Who will I be when I choose happiness?
- ✓ What will I *exclude* from my life in order to be happy?
- ✓ Who and what I would like to *invite* in order to fill my life with happiness?
- ✓ How can I create happy situations?
- ✓ How will my life, filled with happiness, look?

- ➢ Happiness is a choice
- ➢ Happiness is a journey, not a destination
- ➢ Choose *HAPPINESS*

You have to choose happiness
Or
Choose happiness!

5.2 Choose Self-Worth

Sometimes we might forget to consider believing in ourselves. We might forget to realize who we really are as we get busy with life – whether attending to others or just not appreciating who we are.

Many times you might not think too highly of yourself. You might be living with old memories of other people putting you down. You may have believed them and their impression of you, and as a consequence, you are currently living by the standards they perceived you.

Every one has gifts and special traits. Appreciate who you are, who you really are. Think about the things you are doing well in and the things you excel in. Not everyone has the same traits. Some are very unique to you. Every person has to appreciate who he or she is including their unique traits.

If you have doubts or you are not sure of your traits, it would be helpful to make a list of your traits.

Notes to self:

❖ Evaluate who you are and re-program your belief system, if you need to.

❖ Always remember your self-worth.

❖ Live according to your self-worth.

❖ Don't let anyone put you down.

❖ Know your rights and make sure that others treat you with respect.

❖ Respect and demand respect, since you are special.

I often ask my clients when I see that they have no appreciation for their own traits and qualities, to *make a list*, of at least 27[*1] traits and qualities.

---

*1

I have chosen 27 traits as one of my clients suggested to relate it to numerology. The sum of 2 and 7 is 9. Number 9 in numerology represents *"Life purpose," "Soul mission,"* and *"Inner wisdom."*

By: Joanne Walmsley Sacred Scribes
www.numerologythenumbersandtheirmeaningsblogpost.com

The response I get is always, "How can I find so many qualities'? Sometimes, although they don't say it, I can see this question on their face.

My reply is, "Just start. Start with everyday things that you are good at. It can be as simple as "I am gentle to others" or "I love my family," and continue with all that you do well or excel in, at work, at home, and for yourself.

Once they start writing the list, they are amazed to find how the list is taking shape and how easily they find 27 or more of their qualities and traits.

Take a moment and write this list for yourself, it might change your perspective about who you are.

The next step is to read the list and realize how **worthy** you are!

The most important step is to **BELIEVE** that this list is **YOUR** list of traits and qualities.

Celebrate "**YOU**" continually!

Believe and achieve!

- ➤ Self-worth is a choice
- ➤ Appreciate who you are
- ➤ Know your worth
- ➤ Choose *Self-worth*

Count Your Blessings!

5.3 Choose Confidence

Not everyone is born with confidence. Some kids show confidence from the day they are born, and others lack confidence. Some parents encourage and develop confidence in their kids while others are not aware of their children's lack of confidence or have no tools to help to develop it.

People who lack confidence show it in every area of their lives. When you lack confidence, it shows in the way you behave, look, the way you talk to people, and the way you walk.

As you grow and develop, you can develop your confidence. Appreciating who you are is the beginning of gaining confidence. Collecting small victories, one victory at a time, appreciating them, and accepting them as YOUR winnings can help build your confidence. Consider your list of qualities and traits, count each victory in your life, small or big, and appreciate who you are.

You have to demonstrate confidence in all areas of your life, including trusting in yourself. Show and demonstrate your confidence and others will appreciate you more.

I believe that the first step of confidence comes with self-love. Loving yourself and appreciating yourself go hand in hand. When you appreciate yourself and love yourself then your confidence flourishes.

To boost your self-love, I often teach the "mirror exercise." It is a simple exercise that could boost your self-love. You can practice it first thing in the morning and in the evening.

The Mirror Exercise:

Look in the mirror, smile to yourself, and enjoy your smile. Check your smile and your face. Find all things that are beautiful in your face; is it your smile? Maybe your eyes are beautiful? Or is it a gorgeous dimple on your right cheek?

Once you enjoy your smile and your face, say to yourself, "I love you," "I am happy today" and smile more. You can continue and tell yourself, "I love this smile" or any other compliment you want to give yourself. Say, "I love you" a few times. Get used to the idea of loving yourself.

Watch and observe your face, be aware of the love you give yourself, listen to your inner voice, and continue with this exercise.

At first it might feel strange or odd to look at yourself and talk to yourself in the mirror, but in time, you will feel more and more comfortable and loving.

Repeat this exercise twice a day for a period of time; repeat it until you have only nice feelings about it and until you really sense the love you have for yourself.

When you have the confidence to say, "I love myself," "I appreciate myself," and "I value myself," you'll have the confidence to appreciate who you really are and demonstrate it.

- ✓ Work with confidence
- ✓ Behave with confidence
- ✓ Love with confidence
- ✓ Talk with confidence
- ✓ Walk with confidence
- ✓ Dress with confidence

And most important is

Live with confidence!

Enjoy your confident **YOU!**

- ➢ Confidence is a choice
- ➢ Love yourself
- ➢ Appreciate who you are
- ➢ Behave with confidence
- ➢ Enjoy your confidence!

"Women need a supportive environment to live with confidence within yourself. You need to find yourself attractive and that comes from within."

Liz – Fortitude Fitness for Women
www.fortitudewomensgym.com.au

———————————

"People are like stained-glass
windows.
They sparkle and shine when
the sun is out,
But when the darkness sets in,
Their true beauty is revealed
Only if there is light from
within."

Elizabeth Kubler-Ross

———————————

5.4 Choose Peace of Mind

To choose peace of mind, one may ask:
How could I do it? It's not up to me!

But the reality is that we can choose peace of mind. If we eliminate all situations and circumstances that annoy us and upset us, make us angry, distressed, irritated, or furious, we will be left with peace of mind.

Place yourself where you feel safe.

Eliminate situations where you feel fear.

Avoid situations that generate anger and frustration in you.

Give up feelings of guilt, shame, and hurt.

Get rid of negative feelings and judgment.

You might say, "It's impossible to do it" or "I couldn't do it" but the choice is yours; if you want your life to be calm, peaceful, and happy, you have to eliminate all negative feelings.

You have to find the way to solve and resolve old issues, issues that do not serve you and on the other hand are wasting your life and stealing your energy and livelihood.

To eliminate your negative feelings is to:

Forgive yourself and others

When you are busy with stories of relationships that get you upset and are hurting you all the time, you can't find any peace of mind. The movies of those incidents and the strong feelings that you are carrying with you are costing you your peace and happiness.

Forgiveness is the first step to inner peace.

To forgive another person is not always easy and simple. It's not to say that the other person's behavior was or is right. Yes, I know that sometimes it is so hurtful and that you just can't comprehend how you could forgive, especially if it is someone close to you, like a parent, a member of your family, or a very close friend.

What you have to recognize is that the forgiveness is for your own benefit. It is for your own good and peace of mind, especially if you have to forgive yourself. Forgive yourself for things you have done because you didn't know any better or the things you've done because you had to, for your survival or the things you've done because you were young or you just can't explain why you did them.

The important thing is that forgiveness helps YOU! Forgiveness helps you and not necessarily the other person, since you are the one carrying all this hurt and you are the one losing or missing your livelihood and peace of mind. Practice forgiveness, even though it's not always easy and simple, and get YOUR peace of mind.

➤ *Accept people and situations as they are*

All people are different. Some are kind and nice, and some are negative or difficult. We can choose our friends, but we can't choose our family. Make the most of each relationship. Accept people as they are, and if "It doesn't suit you," figure out how to maintain the relationship in a different way or on a different level.

People have their own traits and characteristics. Sometimes we want to change them, to have them behave towards others or us in a different way, but we **can't change anyone**. We have to accept people as they are, even though we may not enjoy their behavior at times. The only thing we can change is the way we react to those behaviors. Your reactions can change how your relationships grow.

When all or most of your relationships are good and enjoyable, you live your life with peace of mind. It is a very simple concept that can change your life.

➢ Embrace positive situations

Embrace and create positive situations that will bring you peace of mind. Avoid situations where you won't find joy or satisfaction. Be the boss of your life and decide the way you want your life to unfold.

Be aware of the energy you bring with you. Always bring with you a positive energy and create joy and harmony wherever you go.

Set yourself FREE

Exercise:

Imagine yourself living your life and along the way, you have different incidents that are very hurtful. Other people are behaving wrongly, hurting you, and you are left broken hearted. Every incident is very hurtful, and you think about it often, talk to people around you, and tell them about your hurt. You carry the hurt and pain.

If you can find a resolution to this conflict, all the pain and hurt can disappear, but if you don't resolve the event that was so hurtful, you'll be carrying the hurt and pain with you for days, months, years, or all your life.

Think about all those incidents in your life that upset you and steal your peace of mind and livelihood.

Imagine each incident or conflict as a big stone. Imagine having a big bag where all those stones are stored. This bag, full of stones, is part of your life, and you are carrying it on your shoulders every day, all day long.

- How heavy is it to carry this bag every day?
- How much of a load are you carrying?

- What would your life look like without this bag?
- How would you feel walking straight and tall, without this bag on your shoulders?

As always in life, you have choices; you can continue to live your life, carrying your bag on your shoulders OR you can take this bag off your shoulders and put it on the ground - put all your hurt and sadness on the ground and leave it there.

It is **YOUR** choice!

What are you choosing **NOW**?

I invite you to make a choice.

I invite you to put YOUR bag on the ground, look at it, say your goodbyes, and continue your life without your "sad" bag.

How will you feel now, walking without carrying your bag?
What would your life look like without carrying any sadness or hurt?

Set yourself **FREE** - try it and create the space – the space for your own peace of mind.

Enjoy your peace of mind!

- ➤ Peace of mind is a choice
- ➤ Eliminate negative feelings
- ➤ Eliminate negative relationships
- ➤ Exclude negative situations
- ➤ Set yourself FREE of negative feelings
- ➤ Enjoy your peace of mind!

*There is harmony
and inner peace
To be found* **everywhere!**

5.5 Choose Success

Success is more than economic gain, titles, and degrees. Planning for success is about mapping out all aspects of your life.

I recognize that success is a big choice. When you talk to people who became millionaires or billionaires, they will tell you that from the start, they decided that they wanted to be successful and they knew that they would.

Success wasn't an option for them it was a choice!

You too, can *choose success*, to be successful in whatever you do.

When you choose success, you choose many objectives that are part of success.

People who choose success don't settle for any other option; they choose to work and do whatever it takes to succeed.

Vision

People who choose success always have a vision. They know exactly what they want to achieve and how they will achieve it. A vision is a must in order to know what you want and how to get it.

Attitude

People who choose success have a certain attitude - a positive attitude, and the attitude of "I can do it" and "I will do it." There is no compromising in their attitude.

Belief

People who choose success believe in their success. They believe in the path they are taking to achieve their success and no one could change their belief.

Commitment

People who choose success have the highest commitment that you'll find. They are committed to their vision, belief, and success! They are committed to never giving up and always persevering. They never allow negative thoughts, fear, or failure interfere with their commitment.

Passion

People who choose success have the passion to achieve it. They are passionate about everything they do. They don't count the hours or the number of days they work. Their passion is the fuel that helps them succeed.

Courage

People who choose success have courage. Usually, they are doing something different from the norm; they are choosing different paths for achieving success. Their paths are not always conventional and they need courage to be different.

They need courage for persevering since not all paths are easy and direct. They need courage to stand tall in difficult situations.

Love

In my mind, the most important ingredient people who choose success, need, is love. They definitely love what they do; otherwise, they wouldn't invest so much of themselves to achieve their success. Their motto is simple: "Love what you do!" They couldn't have done it without love.

Choose success! Enquire and check that you have all the ingredients to achieve it and never give up!

*The definition of success is to live life with more **passion**, more **beliefs**, more **courage**, more **compassion**, more **joy**, more **gratitude**, and especially more **LOVE!***

It's your success, enjoy your path and celebrate your success!

- ➢ Success is a choice
- ➢ Certain essential ingredients are required for success, they are:
  Vision, attitude, belief, commitment, passion, courage and love
- ➢ Add extra ingredients to your success like:
  Compassion, joy and gratitude
- ➢ Enjoy your Success!

What are **YOUR** choices?

What are YOU **choosing** TODAY?

I choose today

_____

Date: _____

The real secret for success Is enthusiasm!

Walter Chrysler

Chapter 6

Predict Your Future

6.1 Dream Big

I often meet people who have aspirations and dreams. They aspire to achieve or accomplish. They don't always have all the details of their dreams figured out and how they will reach them.

At times, I come across people, especially women, who are dreaming about small achievements. They design their dreams on a small "canvas" (the canvas of life), instead of designing them on a large, full-size "canvas." Their dreams look more achievable for them on a small canvas instead of a large one that opens their dreams to the universe.

At my coaching sessions, I often have to encourage clients to get out of their comfort zone into an open space and think big. I inspire them to think about the unthinkable, imagine something huge and wild, and get them to think BIG!

What are your dreams and aspirations?

How **BIG** are your dreams and aspirations?

I encourage you to look at your dreams through a magnifying glass. How big can you make them? How would you look with those big aspirations? And what the results will look like in a large and full-size scale?

If you are anxious or nervous about a big dream, divide it into manageable parts, position those parts one next to each other, like a big puzzle, and create the BIG PICTURE - your big dream! Have the courage to think BIG and DREAM BIG!

Use your inner strength and develop your inspiration to think about your unimaginable BIG dream. Have the courage to make your dream and aspirations bigger, then take them to the next level and make them even BIGGER! Don't hold yourself back and don't be scared to express yourself!

I invite you to **DREAM BIG!**

You have the freedom to dream. Choose the size of your dream and create your BIG DREAM.

And... turn your dream into reality.

A

DREAM

Written with a date becomes a

GOAL

A goal broken down into steps becomes a

PLAN

A plan backed by

ACTION

Makes your dream a

REALITY

- ➢ Think **BIG**
- ➢ Dream **BIG**
- ➢ Believe **BIG**

And your results will be BIG

_____

Your wings always exist,
All you have to do is
Fly!

– – – – – – – – – – – – – – – –

6.2 Trust the Timing of Your Life

Trust the timing of your life. The time is not always right for you to do or achieve, as the time is not always aligned with your schedule. Things don't always happen when you want them to.

Sometimes you try and try to achieve something and nothing happens - you have no results and no success. At other times, opportunities appear but you might not be ready for them, or perhaps they didn't appear at the right time for you.

Occasionally, the universe is planning something different for you, so the right time is not now or the situation might not be right for you.

It reminds me of the time when I finished building my house. The week that I put the house on the market, the government decided to increase the interest rate. That followed by three other interest rate increases, which stopped the real estate market in its tracks. Suddenly, the whole real estate market was at a stand still since people couldn't afford the higher mortgage payments with higher interest rates.

As I planned to sell my house at that stage, unfortunately I couldn't sell the house as the real estate market collapsed in a matter of weeks.

I have tried my best in all different ways to sell it but the market was "dead." There were no buyers available. I tried selling through different agents; I tried to sell it as a private sale but with no results. There were no buyers in the real estate market.

The weeks passed, the months passed, and even the years, and no prospect of any buyers or offers. I was lucky that I didn't buy another house before selling mine, as I would have found myself in dires strait.

But on the other hand, I did not live in that house anymore, but I still had to maintain it constantly, so it wouldn't look vacant. I used to go by at least twice a week to maintain the house and the garden, so it would look like someone lived there.

It took nearly four years for the economic situation to improve. During those four years, I had the option of getting upset, angry, or be depressed about the situation, since it wasn't an easy time and I had no say in the matter.

But I chose to take the philosophical way, and when people asked me if I sold my house, I would reply, "The buyer hasn't arrived yet." Some people looked at me strangely - they couldn't comprehend this concept - but others understood my reply.

I couldn't explain it in any other way. It was not up to me; I felt that there was some other power that was managing it and that it wasn't in my control.

In time, I sold my house to a lovely woman that approached me through my real estate agent, in order to rent my house for a few months and then purchase it. She was in a situation where she sold her house before the collapse of the real estate market in order to build a small complex of apartments for investment.

She got stuck in the same economic period with an inability to sell the apartments. She lived with her young family in a very small house, which she planned originally to be a short-term solution, and she couldn't bare the small living space any longer.

When my house was sold after the renting period, I bought another house from a man that was waiting too for the last four years to sell his house. He had a similar story to mine, trying to sell his house but there were no buyers.

His friend, a real estate agent, convinced him to put an advertisement only on the Internet so he won't have extra advertising expenses and try to sell the house that way. I was lucky enough to find it and was more than happy to purchase it.

That life experience and a few others taught me to trust the timing of my life and that the universe has its ways.

It showed me that sometimes the universe moves in unexplained and unexpected ways and that it's not always up to us, as if someone is somehow managing us with a remote control.

Only later, maybe much later, when you look back, you may see the reasons for the delays or changes that occur in your life.

Similar experiences happen to people who are looking to find a life partner, husband or wife, and to people who are looking to find a job or to buy a house. It's not always up to you; you have to do your utmost in your quest, but if you don't succeed, you have to trust the timing of your life and the universe. The universe has its way.

The universe works to bring you everything you need at the right time. Have faith that everything is happening for you.

- ➢ Trust the timing of your life
- ➢ It's not always up to us
- ➢ Trust the universe
- ➢ The universe has its ways

Everything Happens
For a Reason!

6.3 Make a Decision for a Better Life

If you want something new or different in your life, you have to ask for it, direct your energy to wish for it, and be ready to receive it. Nothing will happen if you just dream of it.

If you want something better in your life, decide that you want it. Acknowledge your wishes. Know what you want exactly, as it is the only way to achieve it. If you don't know what you want, how will you reach it or get it?

Always aim to have and achieve the best – the best things for you, the best your money can buy, or the best achievements you can reach. It can be the best education, the best life partner, furniture, house, or anything your heart desires. Always aim for the best, the best life you can have.

Not everyone has the inclination, aspiration or the ambition to ask for things in their lives. Some women might think of it as ill mannered and selfish. It is not egotistic to ask and aim for a better life, it is your privilege to ask, since the universe has abundance of everything. You should aim for it, if you don't ask, you will never have.

Don't be afraid to aim for the best, to have a better life. It is part of dreaming BIG.

Make a decision that you *want* a better life, as it is very important to have the awareness for a better life and to aim for it. You should have the ambition, courage and aspiration to have a better life and to achieve more.

One of my friends, many years ago, told me to ask for big things, not to be shy about it. "When you want something," she said, "you have to ask for it, ask for it specifically, and not be reluctant about asking for it in a big way."

She used to tell me about her belief that the universe listens to all the people's requests, big and small requests. To the small requests, the universe's reaction is insignificant since they are small, not trivial but minor, and not always granted.

The reaction of the universe to the big requests is very serious since they are big and significant requests. The universe sometimes consents to the whole of the big requests and sometimes to only part of them.

"Always ask for something big", my friend used to tell me, "At least part of it will be granted, if not the whole lot."

- ➢ Make a decision for a better life
- ➢ Don't be scared to aim for a better life
- ➢ Ask for the best
- ➢ Make BIG requests

Make A Decision For
A Better Life,
Your Time Is
NOW!

Chapter 7

Live Your Dreams

7.1 Dream Your Life –
Live Your Dream

We all dream about things we want in our lives. We dream about having more money, starting a business, having a better job, finding a life partner, going on a trip, buying a car, starting a new hobby or sport, or any other wish.

Dreaming is the first step to achieving it.

It all starts in our mind as a

Thought → which develops into an

Idea → and with more details, looks like a

Realistic item → and turns into a

DREAM

Once you have a DREAM, remember to dream BIG!

Dream it in color, dream it with all the details filled in. Imagine you are living your dream: What does it look like? How do you see it? How do you feel achieving it? How will your life look living your dream? Make it a reality in your mind so that it will become a reality in your life.

Your dream can stay as a dream for months, years, or forever. OR you can choose the option to "convert" your dream into reality. When you convert your dream into reality that is when you start to *live your dream.*

185

Whether you have one dream or a few dreams that are kept in your mind or your heart, decide if you want to "convert" them and live them, and then decide when to convert. Plan the timing of when you would like to live your dreams.

Don't leave your dreams dormant. It's not always simple to create and live your dream, not always the right time for it, but it is possible.

Business people are visionaries; they are visionaries who live their dreams. They imagine their dreams long before they have started their business. They can describe their business long before they start it. They can see it as if it does already exist. Once they start their business, they are living their dream.

They are not working even one day; they are just creating their dream.

Be visionary like business people in creating your dream.

Your dream can be a small one or a very big one, but you are the only one that can "convert" your dream from just a dream into your reality. You have the *power* to live your dream.

Share your dream with other people; tell them about your dream and your plans, which will build accountability and inspiration.

People around you can be your biggest supporters. Get inspired by your supporters, they are the positive energy that will celebrate with you in happy moments and help you in difficult moments. Avoid sharing your dream with negative people or people who bring negative thoughts, doubt, or negative energy. Stay with the positive and

FOLLOW YOUR DREAM!

It might take days, weeks, months, or even years to achieve it, but in the end, the achievement is your achievement: to

Live your dream.

- ➢ Be the author of your life
- ➢ Dream your life
- ➢ Dream BIG, and add color and details to it
- ➢ "Convert" your dream into reality
- ➢ It is always possible!
- ➢ Live your dream

"The biggest regrets in life we have,
are the risks we never took.
You have to be resilient."

Rosie Shalhoub – Embrace - Psychic, Clairvoyant, Astrology
www.embraceaustralia.com.au

Live your dreams,
They know the way!

7.2 Discover the Person You Dream To Be

Some people are not really happy with who they are. They have thoughts about the person they would have loved to be. They dream about this person. They might not be happy about one or more aspects of their lives, but they don't always have the impulse to reach and become the person they really dream to be.

Just to clarify, you are perfect the way you are! There is nothing wrong with you. Maybe you would like to change some aspects of your life, as you might dream to be different in some way or to improve your qualities and traits. Traits can be: compassion, courage and loyalty, helpful or imaginative.

To discover the person you dream to be, you have to gain more insights about yourself. You need to look closely at your beliefs, values, and principles. In order to create your vision, reflect on your experiences and think about the person you dream to be.

Know yourself so that you have a clearer idea of who you want to be, and the things you wish to amend or fine-tune, like attitudes, habits, or point of views. Recognize those areas so that the vision of who you want to be will be clearer.

Discover and define the areas of your life that you wish to improve. Make a list and set the steps to become that person. If you wish to be more helpful, offer your help whenever you see or hear of a person in need. It can be as simple as helping an old lady to carry her shopping or to cook a meal for a sick friend. Maybe you want to be more courageous, try and do things you have never tried before, because you were cautious or scared to do them.

You can start with baby steps, like choosing to drive each day a different route to work or home, to discover the unknown or choose to leave your fear at home, and do things you never dared doing before.

There are many things you can do in order to improve your traits or decide you wish to have new traits. If you were not sociable lately, you can decide now, that you wish to be more sociable. Take the steps to be more sociable, initiate gatherings of friends, call your friends and enjoy your new or improved YOU.

You can always improve your traits, character, and behaviour, but you cannot be anyone else.

Be honest with yourself, be authentic, and BE the person you *dream to be.*

➤ You are perfect!

➤ There is nothing wrong with you!

➤ You can improve your qualities and traits

➤ Discover the areas of your life that you wish to improve

➤ Take the steps to improve your traits, start with baby steps

➤ Be the person you dream to be

You don't have to be perfect
To be Amazing!

7.3 "Be Yourself;
Everyone Else Is Taken"

Oscar Wilde

Be yourself. Be the person you wish and plan to be. Don't copy anyone else and don't aspire to be anyone else. Be true to yourself; be true to who you really are.

Don't compare yourself to anyone else, as there is no comparison. You are unique; there has never been another person like you, and there is no one else in the world like you. So there is no reason to compare yourself to others.

You might compare yourself to others and feel superior, and that is only to put someone else down, to feel better than them. Or you might compare yourself to others and think that you are not as good, but that only elevates others while putting yourself down. Comparison is a path that has neither justification nor any meaningful results, since everyone is special and unique in their own way.

Sometimes when you compare yourself to others, you forget to shine the light on yourself, to show the world who you really are, to shine the light on all your unique qualities that make you such a special person.

Imagine an apple tree. The tree is full of apples; the branches are carrying an abundance of beautiful and juicy fruit.

Come a bit closer and look at the apples. Some are green and some are red. Some are big, some are small, some are round, and some are shiny. They all look so beautiful and juicy, but when you look closer, you can see that no apple is like any other on the tree. They all have their own unique look, but they are all sweet and juicy. Can you compare them?

You might have your preference - maybe you like a smaller apple or a rounded one – but that does not make one apple better than the other, since they are all delicious apples that give nutrition and good taste.

These apples are exactly like us, people. We are all people with our special uniqueness.

- ➢ Be yourself!
- ➢ Be true to who you really are
- ➢ Don't compare yourself to others

"Surround yourself with like minded people,
the type of person you want to become
and be the best version of yourself."

Kylie – Judea Hair
www.judeahair.com.au

The freedom to be yourself,
is a gift,

Only YOU
can give yourself

Chapter 8

Celebrate "YOU"

8.1 Know Your Value

Many of my coaching clients often thank me for introducing them to the concept of "know your value." It is *not* always a model that people are aware of or thinking about it, day to day.

Every person has value; some values are very important like the value of being a parent, son or daughter, spouse, friend, worker, colleague, or partner.

Others include our value as part of our profession, what we are doing, and whom we are helping or serving. Another aspect is the value of who we are as people, as human beings.

We all have value, and it is very important to know this. Your value can also be your qualities and traits, your achievements, and your service to society.

You might not ever think about the value you have and bring to your surroundings or what it means to others. Every person has value, and everyone should know and appreciate his or her own value.

Your value comes from what you are doing in your life and the way you enrich other people's lives, organizations, or the world around you.

When you know your value, you behave with self-esteem, respect to yourself and others and confidence. You appreciate who you are and what you are bringing to the table.

Never let other people diminish or lessen your value; know your value in order to behave with confidence and respect. When you know your value, you appreciate yourself first. You have the understanding to be confident and appreciate who you are.

- ➢ Every person has value
- ➢ Know your value
- ➢ Appreciate your value
- ➢ Confidence and self-esteem are results of knowing your value

Show your essence!

8.2 Appreciate Who You Are

Many times we think negatively and concentrate on our limitations. We think of what is not working in our lives, and about our negative beliefs "I can't," "It won't work," 'It's impossible," and "It's not for me."
Somehow, along the way, we forget to appreciate who we are, who we really are.

I would like to remind you always to remember who you are. Remember all your traits; remember your qualities and your uniqueness. We always have to appreciate the qualities we bring with us. We have to appreciate the goodness, intelligence, our wisdom, uniqueness and all other qualities we have and the way they shine through us.

At difficult times or at a time of distress or doubt, don't give your negative feelings a chance to rise to the surface. Instead bring into your conscious mind your appreciation of who you really are. Have your list of unique traits and qualities close by, and remember to read them from time to time to remind yourself to appreciate the reasons why you shine.

My clients often tell me about incidents in their lives where they regain confidence to manage or succeed in certain situations, especially when they reminded themselves of "who they are."

They shared the knowledge of appreciating their qualities of being nice, clever or courageous, gave them a boost of confidence to stay strong in situations where they had to be powerful and brave, to stand on their rights, and not let anyone win over them.

Remind yourself that **you are** a

Strong, clever, good, talented, gentle, nice, smart, beautiful, powerful, influential, confident, passionate, courageous, inspiring, delicate, appreciative and intelligent woman.

The list doesn't end here. You can add more of your qualities to that list. Lean on it, and never forget who you are or the qualities that shine through you every moment.

ALWAYS appreciate who you are!

203

Two friends were walking in the desert. While crossing a vast area of sand dunes, an argument broke out between them.

One of the friends slapped the other one in the face. The one that received the slap became very upset, and without saying a word wrote on the sand:

"My best friend slapped me in my face today."

They continued on their way in the desert until they arrived to an oasis with a waterhole and decided to wash themselves.

The guy who was slapped by his friend suddenly started to sink in the mud around the waterhole. His friend saw what was happening and hurried to save him.

Following his recovery, he engraved on a stone:

"My best friend saved my life today."

His friend looked at him and asked, "After I slapped you in the face, you wrote on the sand, but now you engrave this on the stone. Why is that?"

The guy replied,

"When someone hurts us, we have to write it on the sand so the *wind of forgiveness* will be able to erase it. But when someone saves us or treats us especially well, we should engrave it on a rock *so no wind* will be able to erase it."

Learn to write your hurts on sand and engrave your goodness and blessings on a stone.

- ➤ Appreciate who you are
- ➤ Always remember who you really are
- ➤ Remind yourself the qualities that shine through you

*"You have to be grateful for all
you have got in life.
Look on the bright side and keep positive."*

Joh Bailey – Joh Bailey, Hairdressing
www.johbailey.com.au

Today you are you.
That is truer than true.
There is no one alive
Who is YOUER than YOU.

Dr. Seuss

Chapter 9

Get That Little "EXTRA" (extraordinaire) and... SHINE!

9.1 Go with an Open Heart

To be able to achieve all the "richness" in life, you have to go with an open heart. Fill your heart with love and compassion, see the positive in everything, and enjoy being able to breathe with ease and joy while enjoying your life.

Going with an open heart is including acceptance - accepting people as they are, accepting who you are, and accepting that sometimes "it is what it is."

Accepting and embracing life as it comes, means accepting the low points and the high points in life, knowing that there is a reason and timing for everything.

Go with an open heart, even if it doesn't make sense to you at times, trust that there is order in the world and that everything happens for a reason.

One day the professor entered his class and told the students that he decided to give them a test that day. The students were surprised to hear about this test. They sat quietly and waited for the papers to be distributed.

The professor passed the papers; he put them on the student's desks with the text facing down, as he always did with tests. When he finished distributing the tests, he asked his students to turn over the papers.

The students hurried to turn the papers over and, to their surprise, there were no questions on the paper. The only item they saw was a black dot in the middle of the page.

The professor didn't wait to see the students' reaction and said, "This test will not be considered for your end of year marks. Please write and describe what you see on the page."

The confused students looked for a while at the paper and eventually started to write about the vague task. At the end of the test, the professor collected the test papers, and without waiting, he started to read aloud the descriptions the students wrote.

209

All the students, without fail, described the black dot by trying to explain the position of the dot in the center of the page.

When the professor finished reading aloud, the confused class went quiet and the professor started to explain, "I don't intend to discuss your explanations. I was only interested in giving you something to think about. No one wrote about the large area of white on the paper. Everyone was concentrating on the black dot. And it is the same in life; we have a large white paper, but we always choose to see the dark stains.

Our life was given to us as a present with love, and we always have reasons to celebrate; nature is renewing itself each and every day, we have friends around us, and our work provides us with income and a livelihood. Yet we choose to look at the dark spaces, the black spot; health problems that bother us, shortage of money, relationships that go sour, or a disappointing friend.

Those dark spots are very small compared to all that we have and have achieved in life, but they are staining our minds. Look away from the dark spots in your life. Enjoy each and every bright light: they take up the majority of space in your life.Enjoy the beautiful light spots that life spreads around you, and live a full life with love and joy."

210

Going with an open heart it's all about acceptance and trust. Trust and believe in whatever you believe in – knowing that you have done the best you could.

BELIEVE - ACCEPT - EMBRACE - TRUST - ENJOY

- ➢ Go with an open heart
- ➢ Accept people as they are
- ➢ Accept who you are
- ➢ "It is what it is"
- ➢ Practice:

  Believe - Accept - Embrace - Trust – Enjoy

———————————

Allow things to come and go,
Keeping your heart as open
As the sky

Lao Tzu

9.2 Count Your Blessings

I have been talking about it for years, training my clients to look on the positive side and not the negative side. With my positive attitude, I always look at the positives and try to forget all the negatives that steal our livelihood from us.

I have found that, rather than dwelling on the negative, if you can take a step back and consider the blessings in your life, including the seemingly small, which were sometimes overlooked, you will find *greater happiness.*

Be grateful for what you have and for what you don't have. To remind yourself of all the blessings you have in your life, you can create:

"The blessing list"

"The blessing list"

Exercise:

On a piece of paper write a list of all your blessings. Write the small blessings and the big ones, as they are equally important. Think of all the blessings you receive every day, at home, at work, with your family, and elsewhere.

Write the blessings you are given and the blessings you get back when you contribute to others.

Blessings can be, big and important, like a good family, a loving spouse, enjoyable and healthy children, a successful profession, a special friend, happiness, good health, caring parents, a good memory, and so many more.

Smaller blessings can be a hobby you enjoy, a nice smile, or an enjoyment of the outdoors, the ability to swim, the pleasure of reading books, nice handwriting, and many others.

Make a list of all your blessings and prioritize them; the top blessings should be the most important blessings to you. You can easily have 50 or 100 blessings.

Copy them onto a nice piece of paper and keep it handy, somewhere where you can see it daily. Appreciate what you have!

Let me encourage and inspire you to get up every day and focus on what you have in your life. Check your "blessing list" if you need extra inspiration. Be thankful for each and every blessing you have in your life.

Enjoy the little things, because one day you may wake up and discover that they were the big things.

Once you realize how valuable you are and how much you have going for you, the smiles will return, the sun will shine, the music will play, and you will be able to move forward in your life with courage, confidence, strength, and grace.

Beginning today, make it a habit to count your blessings everyday.

- ➤ Count your blessings!
- ➤ Count your big blessings and your small ones
- ➤ Create your "blessing list"
- ➤ Be grateful for each and every blessing in your life
- ➤ Move forward with courage, confidence, and grace

Count your blessings
And make your blessings count!

Treat yourself as gold.
Live your truth.
Express your love.
Share your enthusiasm.
Make your choices count.
Take action toward your dreams.
Walk your talk.
Dance and sing to your music.
Make a decision for a better life.
Be yourself.
Count your blessings.
Just SHINE!

Epilogue

Throughout the year 2019 and beginning of 2020, *Strong Women Finish Rich* became a big part of my life. Over the years, while coaching and mentoring many women, I have gathered the many lessons, stories, wisdom, tools and creativity, which I used and enabled them to transform and flourish.

Strong Women Finish Rich is both deeply personal and based on a large amount of knowledge, experience, materials and tools. In writing this book, I drew on the knowledge of coaching, mentoring and personal development, topped with creativity of tools, stories and poems, to create memorable insights and change in clients.

I remember when I couldn't paint very well. The first painting lesson I went to was a class of experienced painters. They had been attending this class for a while and were at a higher level of painting.

At my first lesson, the teacher gave us an exercise to paint some tools that she had put on a table. I looked at the tools and looked at the other students who started to draw and paint with enthusiasm, and I didn't know where to start.

I struggled at this session and tried my best, but the results were less than desirable. I was upset with my results, especially compared to the other students in the class.

At the end of the class, the teacher approached me and said that she would like to give me a specific exercise at the next lesson, to see if painting was for me. (I got the impression that she didn't think much of my painting abilities.)

I arrived to the following lesson, and the teacher gave me a special project to do. I was given a small canvas and was instructed to divide it into nine squares. I also had to divide a photocopy of a painted picture into nine squares, and then copy and paint each individual square of the picture onto the squares of the canvas, painting each square in a different style, which I had to research in books.

The results were just beautiful; it was my first steps in learning about painting, and it seemed like the art teacher had the assurance that I could draw and paint.

221

Many years later, my paintings have been displayed in various exhibitions, including the "Clio Art Fair" exhibition in New York.

This is a story about a hidden gift that I discovered later in life. We all have many gifts that we were born with but sometimes they are hidden. At times, someone has to direct us into the path of discovery - to find those gifts and let them shine!

I have shared with you in this book, my thoughts and ideas, to direct you into the path of discovery and achievement. Some ideas are inspirational, some are simple and some are more complex. When you take a closer look at them, I hope that the overriding reaction (emotion) is one of inspiration, feeling that you too are capable of being a strong and rich woman.

What is a "rich woman" for you now, after reading this book?

Can you see yourself as a *"rich woman"*?

Is a rich woman a woman rich in money, assets, and possessions, or is it having a rich life like:

A strength of character – resilient

A loving life with family and friends

A happy life

A peaceful life

A life filled with joy

A successful life

An enjoyable and rewarding job

A life filled with satisfaction

And

A life filled with LOVE?

Whatever it is for you, *Enjoy your rich life!*

As the title of this book demonstrates, you can be a strong woman. The real driver of success is simply *implementation* – your ability to put into practice and take action. Implementation is re-reading, planning, imagining and applying until it becomes part of you.

To get the most out of the ideas and insights of this book, review each chapter, and at the end of each chapter answer the following questions:

- *What is the most important insight I got from this chapter?*

- *How can I implement this concept into my life, starting today?*

- *What is my biggest new insight?*

In order to get the full benefit out of your new understandings and insights, write them down. Keep them where you can see them often: next to your bed, on your desk, or next to your computer. They will be your *"reminders"* to keep you on the path towards being a strong and rich woman.

TODAY is your starting point! Take this book's ideas along with your insights, dream BIG, and put them into action; watch yourself emerge as a strong and rich woman.

You are reminded, *in case your mind is playing tricks on you today:*

You matter

You're important

You're loved!

I give you permission to be all that you can be!

NOW is the right time to open yourself up to the potential of receiving all the good and abundance in the world!

To your success,

Edna Ferman xx

The Power
Is
Within
YOU!

Appendix A

Life Concepts

- ➤ Respect everything you have done!
- ➤ Don't look back; you are not going that way.
- ➤ Your wings already exist; all you have to do is fly.
- ➤ If it costs you your peace, it's too expensive.
- ➤ Learn the lesson; turn the page.
- ➤ You never fail until you stop trying. - Albert Einstein
- ➤ Prioritize experiences that bring you joy.
- ➤ Woman, who knows what she wants, usually gets it!
- ➤ Think BIG, Dream BIG, Believe BIG and the results will be BIG.
- ➤ Keep some room in your heart for the unimaginable
- ➤ Count your blessings.
- ➤ Be grateful.
- ➤ Give generously.
- ➤ Embrace change.
- ➤ Yes you can!
- ➤ Give yourself permission to SHINE.
- ➤ The power is within YOU!

*Your future depends
On many things...
Mostly
YOU!*

Appendix B

 # My Instant Self-esteem Booster

Walk
A walk of a minimum of 45 minutes, out in nature,
will change your mind set and your mood for
the whole day.

Exercise
Exercise 2 or 3 times a week. Your body and mind
will love you for that.

Be calm
Accept everything in a calm and easy manner.

Practice kindness
Be kind to yourself and others. Treat yourself with
kindness – you are the most important person
in your life.

Listen to your heart
Listen to what your heart desires, your feelings are
always right.

Enjoy the NOW
Enjoy what you are doing at each moment. Don't bother with the past or think about the future when you are busy with NOW!

Laugh a lot
Find people, books, movies, shows and situations, that make you laugh.

Love as much as you can
Love as much as you can - you will get so much more in return.

Let's Have More Strong Women!

My goal for this book is to inspire thousands and maybe millions of women to be strong and to have extraordinary lives.

I invite you to spread the message and help me inspire as many women as you can. Keep up the conversation by joining the Facebook group "Strong Women Finish Rich" or the Facebook page: www.facebook.com/ednafermancoaching.

If you would like to engage with me, have a question, suggestion, story to share or request a talk or presentation, you are invited to contact me:

Email: edna@ednaferman.com

Website: www.ednaferman.com

Facebook:
www.facebook.com/ednafermancoaching

Facebook group: Strong Women Finish Rich

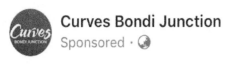

Acknowledgements

My deepest thanks go to the many people who believed in the idea of the book and gave me so much support and encouragement.

❖ A special thanks to all my past and present coaching and mentoring clients, with whom I shared, and through them I developed new coaching insights and new creative tools, to enable them to have lasting positive outcomes, which was the core of the creation of this book.

❖ My love and special thanks to my Mum Rina and my Dad the late Dan Yancovitch, for their dedication, love, and support – always.

❖ To my Mum, your great support, love, and passing me your strength of character, generosity and creativity, enriching my life in every step of the way.

❖ To my Dad, thanks for passing me the love of math and numbers, but above all, your great belief in me, and your special love will always be treasured.

❖ My love and special thanks to my partner Alexander (Alan) Rubel for the love, support and patience, enabling me to embrace myself in writing this book and follow my dreams.

❖ My love and special thanks to my children, Shirley Ferman and Roy Ferman. Thank you so much for being such an important and joyful part in my life. Thanks for all the lessons, experiences, enjoyment and your support that enriched me and contributed to my knowledge and understanding of life. In addition, special thanks to Shirley's assistance with the absolute final proof reading of this book.

❖ My love and deepest thanks to my brothers, Gidi Yancovitch and Guy Yancovitch for giving me their unconditional love and support always.

❖ A special thanks and love to my daughter in law, Rochel Ferman, for her input, suggestions and assistance in creating the name of the book that have made it such a powerful one.

❖ My love and gratitude to my very special friend Helen Sher, I am profoundly grateful for all her help. When I offered her to read the manuscript, she turned and offered editing the book. Helen edited the last version of the book with great edits, feedback, suggestions, and input, with love, grace, and dedication to every detail. Her input is invaluable.

❖ I am thankful that my dear friend Edna Schur-Rubinstein, CEO, Founder and Visionary of Re-Source Institute International, generously gave her time to provide an excellent Forward for this book. I have long known Edna, her remarkable work and career, and it is an honor to include her invaluable words.

❖ My love and deep thanks to all my close and extended family, friends and followers in Australia and around the world, who support and encourage me constantly with their love and kind words.

❖ My deepest gratitude goes to Black Card Solutions; to Gerry Robert for moving me forward to create the book I had in me and was waiting to come out. My sincere thanks to Daisy Gamboa for her guidance and support. I live my life with your motto:
"Make Today The Best Day Of Your Life."

❖ My deepest gratitude and thanks to my sponsor, for her utmost support, who believed in me and in my book, long before it was ready for publishing:

Leilani (Lei) Que - Curves Bondi Junction

❖ Many thanks and great appreciation to all business owners, who agreed to be interviewed for the book, their life philosophies can be found throughout the book.

❖ And finally, to the reader: to YOU, most of all,

THANK YOU!

NOTES

1. **Systemic work** is a powerful healing method, understanding of loyalties within family members, and as a result, holding onto emotions and pains from our ancestors into our generation and story, that affects us on an epigenetic level.

All tales, fables and stories are based on folktales:

ABOUT THE AUTHOR

Edna Ferman - Author, Speaker and a Transformational Life Coach for women. After a successful commercial business career, she established her coaching profession. Edna was the presenter of numerous workshops and seminars for women, and is the author of "Goals4Success," and "Shine" E-books. In addition, to her coaching, she is a painter, her creativity is expressed in her coaching, writing and in her abstract paintings. Edna was born and grew up in Israel, she lives in Sydney, Australia.

Printed in Great Britain
by Amazon